Praise for **Stop Second-Guessing Yourself— Baby's First Year**

"Thank goodness for Jen Singer: She'll talk you down off the ledge of parenting, then make you laugh and actually enjoy this crazy time."

—Sarah Smith, senior editor, *Parenting* magazine

"For mothers wondering whether they're the only ones who find birthday parties a nightmare and getting out the door impossible, *Stop Second-Guessing Yourself* is a lifeline. Jen Singer weaves together pages and pages of practical advice, funny stories, and insights. Her mixture of humor, reality, and compassion will give all moms a lift."

—Kate Kelly, managing editor, *American Baby*

"Jen Singer's books are full of great advice to help moms conquer the toughest job in town—parenting. In fact, she's been my own potty whisperer! They say it takes a village to raise a child, but Jen has managed to gather all the town's mothers and pass along great advice for us all."

—Melissa Joan Hart, actress

"Jen Singer gets it! Finally, someone who truly understands what parents are going through. Take a break from the insanity and read Jen's book. It's laugh-out-loud funny and jam-packed with parenting tips that really work!"

—Juli Auclair, host, *Parents TV*

"Just when you need it most, Jen Singer's books help remind you that laughter and a sense of humor are essential to parenting."

—Charlene Prince Birkeland, parenting editor for *Yahoo! Shine* and founder of crazedparent.org

STOP SECOND-GUESSING

YOURSELF

Baby's First Year

A Field-Tested Guide
to Confident Parenting

Jen Singer

Health Communications, Inc.
Deerfield Beach, Florida
www.hcibooks.com

Library of Congress Cataloging-in-Publication Data

Singer, Jen, 1967-
    Stop second-guessing yourself—baby's first year : a field-tested guide to
confident parenting / Jen Singer.
        p. cm.
    At head of title: Mommasaid.net presents
    Includes index.
    ISBN-13: 978-0-7573-1467-4
    ISBN-10: 0-7573-1467-8
        1. Infants—Care. 2. Infants—Development. 3. Parent and infant. I. Title.
    II. Title: Mommasaid.net presents.
    HQ774.S55 2010
    649'.122—dc22
                                                                    2009040622

Publisher: Health Communications, Inc.
            3201 S.W. 15th Street
            Deerfield Beach, FL 33442–8190

Cover design by Justin Rotkowitz
Interior design and formatting by Lawna Patterson Oldfield

For Omi

Contents

Acknowledgments

Thanks to Allison Janse, editor and visionary, who e-mailed me one day and said, "How'd you like to write some books based on MommaSaid.net?" Your clever insight, superb editing, and unwavering loyalty when, in the middle of the whole thing, I got cancer, will be forever appreciated. Thanks to everyone at HCI for making this book series possible.

Thanks to Wendy Sherman and Ed Albowicz for your hard work, guidance, and friendship. Thanks to Robin Blakely for turning out magic and for your continued support and love. Thanks, too, to Jenna Schnuer and Mark Stroginis for your work behind the scenes.

Thanks to my family: my mom and dad, my brother, Scott, all of my in-laws, especially Omi, who made the baby years easier to handle, plus my nieces and my nephew.

Thanks to my husband, Pete, for continuing to be my biggest cheerleader and my best friend. And to our kids, Nicholas and Christopher, who fill my days with joy and laundry.

Thanks to my doctors, Julian Decter and Alison Grann, who helped return me to health (and hair).

Finally, thanks to MommaSaid's bloggers and our community of parents who help make it a fun place to visit and who so graciously shared many fantastic tips and thoughts throughout this book.

Introduction

I have a confession to make: I don't like babies all that much. Don't get me wrong, I *loved* my babies, and I'm certain that your baby is absolutely adorable. But both of my babies had colic; one of them even cried upward of ten hours a day. Neither slept particularly well for what felt like a decade, and my younger son had reflux, which hurt his belly on and off until he was ten months old and made me feel like an inadequate mother because I couldn't cure it. As a result, my first year of motherhood and my younger son's babyhood were, let's say, not the happiest years of my life. And yet, I learned a lot about caring for babies—and for myself.

My mother-in-law, on the other hand, adores babies. When she found out that I didn't feel quite the same way, she implored, "But they *need* you." I replied, "I really don't want someone to need me so much that I have to pull my car over every few hundred feet to make sure his bobbing head isn't cutting off his ability to breathe."

I had enough of that in college, thank you very much.

So I had to find ways to deal with hours of relentless crying while worrying that I was a lousy mother, even though I knew I hadn't caused my baby's colic or reflux. And I had to navigate the new twenty-first-century motherhood, where we were suddenly supposed to make "teachable moments" out of a trip down the produce aisle and build our babies' brains to prepare them for Harvard or the White House or whatever. And yet, all the previous generations of babies had done just fine without listening to Mozart at nap time. Still, I worried I wasn't doing enough for my babies.

Though my kids are tweens now, I still suffer from the scars of their baby years. We were shopping in Target one recent weekend when I heard the unmistakable sound of a newborn crying—it sounds sort of like a cat in pain. I had to rush through the soap aisle to get away from that baby, because his crying was making my hair stand on end in a sort of post-traumatic stress disorder way. But at least I know I'm not the only one who feels like this.

Through the years, the MommaSaid.net community has generously shared war stories, tips, advice, and commiseration when it comes to parenting babies. From what the heck the baby's rash might be to dealing with Hubby's jealousy of or disinterest in anything having to do with, er, waste removal, their "been there, done that" advice will help moms like you, too, whether you're having a rough go of it, or you're happily soaking up all things babyhood.

On these pages, I'll give you the big picture on parenting babies in a way that you haven't seen before. Throughout the book, MommaSaid's readers provide their own mom-tested tips that will prove handy when you're baffled by an umbilical cord stump or trying (read: pleading) to get your baby to sleep through the night.

It's like we're meeting at the proverbial back fence and, mom-to-mom, going through all the things that keep us up at night when it comes to babies (you know, besides Baby), from spit-up to milestones to how in the world to use that nose-suctioning thing.

You might have a different experience with certain aspects of raising babies, and you'll no doubt have your own advice to give to friends who have babies younger than yours. Whether every word is eye-opening or simply a reassuring pat on the back, remember one very important thing while you're parenting babies: you're not the only one going through it, no matter how alone you feel now and then (or perhaps, every day). So when you need a parenting pep talk, read through this handy guide or drop by MommaSaid.net for laughs and validation. But you'll have to hold your own head up. I am *so* done with that.

Okay, I admit it. . . .

"I wish someone had told me that after you have the baby, all the attention goes away from you and toward the baby, even though you still need it!"

—*Michele, Atlanta, Georgia*

Just a minute!

Life with Baby: The Game

START: It's a Boy/Girl!

Your baby scores a perfect ten on the Apgar test. Put down the video camera and move ahead two spaces.	Poopy diaper.	Your baby wakes up to feed about as often as commercial breaks during American Idol. Go directly to Poopy Diaper.

| | Your baby's umbilical stump (yuck!) falls off—finally. Move ahead two spaces. | Your baby gives up pacifier, but discovers thumb. Move back one space. | | More strained peas wind up on your shirt and in your hair than in baby's mouth. Move back two spaces. |

| | Hubby does the laundry while you nap. Move ahead one space. | You have a dozen tiny socks with no matches. Go back two spaces. | | Baby evades stomach flu—and so do you. Go directly to next Nap Time. |

Baby snoozes five minutes in the car and now refuses to nap in the crib. Move back one space.

Baby joins "Baby Einstein" fan club, and you get to read the entire newspaper! Go to Nap Time.

Nap Time.

Nap Time.

Baby crawls . . . . backward under the couch when you're not looking. Go back to Poopy Diaper.

Sitter doesn't show—and you already paid for the concert tickets. Move back two spaces.

Baby waits for you to come home before creating the blowout diaper of the year. Move back two spaces.

Nap Time.

Baby takes first steps in front of entire birthday party, ten video cameras, and your mom, who's visiting for the weekend. Go to finish.

FINISH: Baby's first birthday.

Chapter One

You Mean, I'm in Charge Now?
Adjusting to Motherhood
One Diaper at a Time

Three days after I brought my son, born five weeks early, home from the neonatal intensive care unit, we were socked with a spring storm that piled eight inches of heavy, wet snow atop our house, the yard, the street, and the wires outside. As a result, the power went out, oh, about every time I needed to feed my newborn. No problem, right? I'll just nurse him in the dark. Except I was using an electronic breast pump because my preemie had gotten his share of bottles in the hospital and, like a fraternity boy during rush week,

Okay, I admit it. . . .

"I sobbed like a baby myself that this tiny bundle of girl depended on me for her sustenance and for the steady hands that would not drop her on her head!"

—Joanna, Bethesda, Maryland

1

preferred to chug. No matter how much I tried to get him to latch on to my breast, he wanted nothing to do with it, fussing and crying through power outage after power outage. And frankly, I cried, too.

Every time the power came back on, I'd rush to pump some more breast milk before . . . *poof!* The power went back out. Then I'd call my husband at work from our bedroom, where the only landline phone in the house is located, and ask him to find out if it's safe for our newborn to sit aside a fire in the fireplace with me. Then I'd call again to ask him where the matches were. Then the power would come back on, and I'd hang up after shouting something about "breasts" and "electricity" and "damn tired," a combination I'm sure he never imagined his wife would utter back when he got down on one knee to propose marriage.

Eventually, the snow melted, and the power stayed on long enough for me to pump enough breast milk to get us through the afternoon. When it was all over, I laughed about it, but when I was in it, I was frazzled. There was nothing in the baby care books called "Pumping Breast Milk During a Freak Spring Blizzard." But I'm not sure how I could have prepared myself, anyhow, outside of installing a generator in the yard. When it comes to parenting babies, sometimes you just have to wing it. Other times, though, it helps to have a heads-up from someone who's been there.

My brother's wife was that someone. Allison had become a mother just sixteen months before me, and she'd already endured colic (clearly, it's in my family's genes) and mysterious rashes and figuring out which way the diaper goes on. When I brought

Nicholas home from the NICU, Allison told me that I was lucky because the nurses had put my newborn on a feeding schedule—a feeding schedule that he ditched his very first night at home in favor of wailing every ninety minutes. Yet Allison proved to be a big help many times when I was confused, lost, or just plain weepy from postpartum hormones.

Whether you have your own Allison or you're pretty much on your own to figure it all out, no doubt you're dealing with the smack upside the head that is

Okay, I admit it. . . .

"I felt like I forgot everything from the baby books I'd read prior to delivery."

—*Kasia, Santa Clarita, California*

going from not being a mother to being a mother or from adding a baby to your growing brood. What's a momma to do?

It worked for me!

"Just take it moment by moment. You are new at this, and so is your new baby!"

—*Kathy, Blountville, Tennessee*

Oh, My God! I *Am* the Mother!

I don't think that the enormity of new motherhood hit me until I nearly called my mother in tears as my newborn's colic began to set in for the very first of about a hundred very long nights to come. I couldn't calm him (or me) down, and my husband was away on a business trip. Alone, scared, and frantic, I thought about calling my mother at 11:00 at night for advice. But before I could reach for the phone, an overwhelming thought came over me. I blurted out, "I can't call my mother. I *am* the mother!"

A few years (and two colicky babies) later, I got a phone call from my neighbor Janet soon after she had brought her own first-born home from the hospital. I heard the baby wailing as soon as I picked up the phone. Janet barked, "Come over here and tell me if this baby has colic!"

I knew how she was feeling. She wanted to know if she was going crazy or if the incessant, inconsolable crying she was enduring really was as bad as it seemed. If I deemed it colic, it meant that she wasn't a miserable failure as a mother. I knew from the frightened tone of her voice and the baby's panicked crying in the background that it probably was colic, but I went next door to check it out anyway. I proclaimed her newborn colicky and then sneaked back home to air out my nervous system.

I had become Janet's go-to mom.

I'll get to the basics of baby care in the early days of motherhood in Chapter 2, but first, I want to give you the same reassurance that I gave Janet: becoming a mother can indeed feel like you've been blindsided by a 1972 Buick Electra. (I know, because I have been blindsided by a 1972 Buick Electra—and also by the demands of motherhood. They produce the same feelings.) And yet, there's likely something that's going to continue to make you doubt yourself and your mothering skills. Somebody, somewhere—whether it's a relative, friend, neighbor, or a posse of moms on the Internet—will seemingly have no problems dealing with motherhood, as though they were born for the job. They will make it look easy with their fuss-less babies and their ridiculously quick return to their prepregnancy weight and their lack of circles under their eyes.

A good friend of mine appeared to be one of these mothers. Her daughter, born a few months after my son, slept so much I called her Rip Van Emma. My son? Not so much. It was just one of the many things that ate away at me, along with the baby powder commercials featuring oh-so-perfect moms and happy-happy-happy babies. And then my friend came over one night with Emma, and all that changed.

Her baby had a horrible case of reflux—to the point where every ounce of breast milk or formula she put into her baby came back out. I witnessed one of her baby's regurgitations, and it was *spectacular*, like a cross between Linda Blair in *The Exorcist* and a Las Vegas fountain show. And suddenly, I realized just how hard motherhood actually was on her, even if she was getting plenty of shut-eye at night.

Sure, there will always be moms who breeze through the baby's first year as though it's the easiest thing they ever did. But if you're not one of those moms, or if you ever have moments (or maybe months) where you're doubting your maternal instincts, remember Emma and Janet and me and know that you're not alone.

Okay, I admit it. . . .

"How could I be responsible for this little person? I was attacked by the 'what ifs' for weeks."

—*Liz, Pompton Lakes, New Jersey*

> "One night our daughter just cried and cried. We bottled, burped, diapered, sang, walked, talked . . . to no avail. She later fell asleep in my arms. I guess I knew then that I would never be a perfect mom, but I was already turning into a good one!"
>
> —Kellie, Derby, Connecticut

It worked for me!

Adjust! Adjust!

I once had a tennis instructor who had his own special way of teaching how to handle a ball that comes toward you higher or lower than you had expected. The second it bounced in a way that I wasn't ready to handle, he'd shout in his Russian accent, "Adjust! Adjust!"

That's exactly what you have to do with motherhood. You may have one image in your mind—one that likely involves absent-mindedly humming while you bathe your healthy, sweet baby—only to find out that having a baby isn't exactly how you'd pictured it.

Please don't worry that there's something wrong with you. Remember when you were pregnant and seasoned parents warned you that having kids will "change your life"? You probably thought this simply meant that you'd shop for a minivan and stay home most Saturday nights. It's that, yes, but now you're discovering that it's so much more. Here's what those well-meaning parents were saying between the lines when they warned you of your impending life-changing event:

1. **You're about to have an overwhelming amount of responsibility that, chances are, you're not really ready for.**
If having a baby is one of the most natural things in the
world, how come it feels so darn difficult? It's because
you've got a very short amount of time to learn how to do
an entirely new, time-consuming, and tiring job. Unless
you're a nanny—and even if you are one—having your own
baby 24/7, not to mention for the next eighteen years, can
make you feel like you've gotten in over your head.

What to do? Cut yourself some slack. Parenting is a tough
job indeed, and you really can't know everything there is to
know from a few Lamaze classes and highlighting passages
in *What to Expect: The First Year.* If you could, there
wouldn't be a few bazillion websites and blogs full of mes-
sages from new parents wondering how to do everything
from treating cradle cap (look it up) to purchasing a baby
monitor. You're not alone, just new.

2. **Everyone's going to give you a lot of advice, but not all of it
is useful, let alone welcomed.** There's no one way to parent
a child, as evidenced by the varying, if not contradictory,
advice you'll no doubt get from well-meaning family
members, friends, and nosy old ladies at the supermarket.
Everyone's got their way to take care of a baby, but not
everyone has *your* baby. Only you and Daddy do. You have
to figure out the best way to parent your baby, no matter
what everyone else says.

What to do? Say "thank you" to advice givers, and then do what you think is best. Think of your friends and family as your advisory board. They are there to tell you what they think you should do, but only you can decide what advice works best. Remember, they don't have as vested an interest in the outcome. After all, you're the one with the pediatrician on speed dial and the instructions for installing the car seat spread out on the coffee table. Your baby, your decisions. Allow yourself that much, and the early weeks (heck, years) will go much more smoothly.

3. **You may not find joy in every moment of motherhood.** Surprise! Having a baby can be hard, no matter how many *People* magazine covers there are with the words "Baby Lust" over smiling pictures of celebrity new moms and their newborns. While there are indeed moments of sheer joy and an enduring deep love you've likely never felt before, you will probably wonder at times, "Why isn't this more fun?" And if you pick the wrong online message boards to post that thought, you may find yourself flamed by mommy propagandists who won't stand for anything but positive news about babies.

   What to do? Do not put on a brave face and pretend your life is all puppies and rainbows when it's not. Find yourself another new mom (or several moms) going through the same self-doubt and disillusionment as you, or a mom with older kids who will tell it to you straight. For me, that mom was my own mom, who was quick to point out that she didn't really care for mothering until my brother and I were old enough to throw a ball with her. (Thanks for being honest, Mom! Also, for teaching me to throw.) You can find someone in your own circle of friends or on your block, but be careful how you broach the subject. A great place to find someone whose feelings match yours is online, either in a social network where moms share their true feelings or on a blog where a brave soul tells it like it is.

4. **Acts of spontaneity will take a very long break.** It's not that you're never again going to be able to, say, decide at 7:00 PM to run out and see a 7:15 R-rated movie. It's that it's probably not going to happen again until your kids are old enough to join you or when Grandma takes the kids overnight, whichever comes first. And while it's a small sacrifice to make for the great benefits of raising children, it does take some getting used to, especially when your kids are little. You can't just shout, "Everybody in the car!" and expect adequate results until your kids are old enough to, at the very least, put on their own shoes and seat belts. And that's a few years off for you.

   What to do? First, plan well. If you've always got the diaper bag packed and ready to go, you won't have to spend ten minutes stocking diapers, refilling wipes, and tracking down pacifiers when it's time to head to the park or Target or even down the street. Second, schedule in some kid-free time, when you can just grab your purse and head out the door in a flash. It'll feel good to be free of all that baby gear, and it'll recharge you for when you're on baby duty and your spontaneity is on hold again.

5. **You're gonna be really, really tired.** If you're not, I don't want to hear about it. Sure, some parents get lucky and wind up with a sleeper. If you're one of those parents, skip to the next section. If not, welcome to the club. My babies didn't sleep much, especially my younger son. I'll go into details on how to fix that sooner than later in Chapter 5 (the lessons I *finally* learned the hard way), but for now, know that for most parents, the early days, weeks, and even months can be very, very tiring. If your baby isn't sleeping, some folks may insinuate that this means you're a lousy parent. While in some cases, your response to a nonsleeper may actually make things worse, for the most part, understand that newborns don't sleep like grown-ups—and that's normal.

What to do? Here's something nobody told me before I had kids: for years, I wouldn't be able to sleep unless everyone else in the house was asleep. Thanks to my husband, I sneaked in a nap on weekends with the cat, who was the only one in the house I could always count on to sleep. But during the week, when I was alone with the kids during nap time, and my husband's pleas of "I've got to work in the morning" trumped my nighttime sleep, I wasn't as fortunate. So, I protected nap time like a dog who growls at anyone who comes near his favorite bone. I made sure we had nap time at roughly the same time each day, and then I napped when they napped. Also, I went to bed right after my babies did, so I could get a few hours in before the nighttime follies began when I'd be up and down, up and down, up and, well, mostly up. To heck with the baby shower thank-you notes and the dishes. It was more important that I rested up whenever I could. Sleep whenever they let you, and you'll feel better. Trust me.

WE ASKED: Was taking care of a baby easier or harder than you thought it would be?

Easier: 25%
Harder: 28%
About what I expected: 44%
I don't remember: 3%

"Sleep when the baby sleeps! Everything else can wait. I didn't listen to this after my first child was born and was doing laundry on day four home from the hospital. It then extended my postpartum recovery."

It worked for me!

—*Michele, Atlanta, Georgia*

"Make sure the episodes of *Oprah* or *Dr. Phil* you watch do not involve any harm to a child, or you will be a weeping basket case by the time Daddy comes home."

—Danielle, Greentown, Indiana

Why Does Everything Make Me Cry?

I remember exactly when the baby blues hit me. I was about to leave my baby in the NICU and go home, because I'd reached my insurance company's forty-eight-hour maximum stay for a vaginal birth. I was pumping milk on an old-fashioned breast pump contraption that looked like it should have released ticker tape with the words, "Allies Defeat Hitler's Army," while my roommate entertained too many guests and her full-term baby on the other side of the curtain. My husband walked into the room to find me crying. "Does it hurt?" he asked. Yes, but not in the way he was thinking.

It was as though I could feel my hormones, which had reached a seemingly all-time high during childbirth, plummet. In fact, they did. Hormones drop precipitously within twenty-four to forty-eight hours after delivery, leaving the vast majority of women with a case of "baby blues." That's why you might burst into tears for no apparent reason (or, in my case, because a mother told her five-year-old son at Party City to "Sit down, Nicholas!" while my Nicholas was still in the NICU). You might get irritable, and you could feel stressed, if not overwhelmed, even trapped, as though this whole motherhood thing might be way too much for you, and perhaps you should just pack it in and call it a day. Only, you can't.

Well-meaning friends and family members might try to remind you that you're "supposed to be happy." They'll tell you that having a baby is a blessing and that you're lucky to be a mother. They may even remind you that not all women are fortunate enough to have babies. In other words, they want you to suck it up. But their reminders, designed to cheer you up, may only serve to make you more miserable, leaving you to wonder what the heck is wrong with you.

The good news is that your hormones will eventually even out, anywhere from ten days to two weeks after delivery when you'll likely feel much better. But a few weeks can feel like an incredibly long, long time, especially if you're awake for much of it. There's not much you can do to speed that up, but you can make it easier on yourself. Here's how:

- **Sleep as much as possible.** This is no time to try to become Supermom. I can't say it enough. You need to rest as much as you can, so your body can recoup from childbirth, which, as comedienne Carol Burnett said, is like "pulling your lower lip over your head." And if you had a C-section, remember that you had *major abdominal surgery,* and then they sent you home to "rest." Ha. The more sleep you can steal, the easier the baby blues will be to take.

- **Ask for help.** You might think, "Women have been doing this for centuries, and so can I." Sure, but for centuries, women had an incredible network of help when they had babies, from grandparents living in the same hut to older children with a lot more responsibilities than filling the dog bowl and starting the dishwasher. It wasn't until the past half-century or so that moms wound up taking the brunt of baby care on their shoulders alone. So, if you can get help—from Daddy, Grandma and Grandpa, the neighbor with bigger kids and a near-daily trip to the supermarket—take it. It'll help you feel less overwhelmed, thereby easing your baby blues symptoms.

• **Talk (or cry) it out.** Don't freak your husband out by wailing incomprehensibly about the TV commercial that set off your nonstop blubbering today. You need to find someone who can handle your emotional instability, preferably someone who will listen without trying to fix it. If that's Hubby, lucky you. But you might want to find another mom or a close friend who'll let you cry it out even if you appear to make no sense at all. Your hormones have taken you hostage, and sleep deprivation is manning the door. Sometimes, all you can do is cry before you'll feel better.

• **Take a break.** It's perfectly okay to leave the baby in the hands of a trusted family member or friend and go wander aimlessly around the mall, or do like I did, nap in the car in the park. Few other jobs or activities require 24/7 attention, and those usually come with some sort of scheduled leave. You not only deserve time off—you *need* it. Even going window shopping can feel like a vacation compared to caring for a newborn. Do it—and enjoy it.

> "Talk to your own mom (if possible) at least once a day, or to another mom you know. It will be reassuring."
>
> **It worked for me!**
>
> —*Emily, San Jose, California*

> "A little bit of meditation and focus away from the baby, a real concerted effort to think of yourself, is extremely important and isn't going to hurt the baby."
>
> **It worked for me!**
>
> —*Amy, Othello, Washington*

When It's More Than Baby Blues

Baby blues usually end after about two weeks. That's not to say that you suddenly start whistling "Don't Worry, Be Happy" while you empty the diaper pail. But it means that your hormones level out, and you start to feel more normal than you have since the baby was born.

But for about 15 percent of women, baby blues turn into post-partum depression. If you experience five or more of these symptoms for two weeks or longer, report them to your ob-gyn:

• Feelings of deep sadness, hopelessness, and/or anxiety

• Loss of pleasure in your everyday activities

• Loss of appetite

- Troubles sleeping, even if your baby is sleeping

- Feeling sluggish (though sleep deprivation will also cause that, so it's a tough call)

- Extreme fatigue

- Feeling worthless or guilty (beyond the usual "I lost the pacifier" mom guilt)

- Problems concentrating (beyond the typical sleep-deprived, hormonal state)

- Thoughts of suicide or of harming the baby

An even more severe concern is postpartum psychosis, which generally begins within three weeks after delivery. Symptoms include:

- Feeling removed from your baby and other people

- Extreme confusion and/or agitation

- Drastic mood changes

- Hallucinations

- Delusional thinking

If you experience any of these symptoms, *seek immediate emergency care.*

WE ASKED: What feelings did you experience when you first brought your baby home from the hospital?

"Wow, she is pretty. When are her parents coming to get her?"

—*Patricia, Kokomo, Indiana*

"We just had a baby, and there was no fanfare. The world kept turning. It didn't make the evening news. And yet, it changed everything forever."

—*Adam, Allentown, New Jersey*

Gimme a break

Don't Blog While Under the Influence of Hormones

Just like friends don't let friends e-mail drunk, avoid blogging, e-mailing, or tweeting while you're awash in hormonally induced mood swings. You might write something you'll regret later when you're better rested and more content with motherhood. Remember, your baby will someday be able to read and surf the Internet. You wouldn't want her to discover that you hated her for an hour or two when she was a colicky baby, would you? Keep your emotions in check when you're at your computer's keyboard. Think before you click.

Just a minute!

Are You Ready for Babyhood?

Practice Test

Comprehension

Read the sample passage and answer the accompanying question.

Karen desperately needs some sleep, but her baby is wailing again. She pads down the hallway, tripping on a pile of unfolded onesies and jumpers and some sort of annoying talking toy. Karen feeds the baby, changes his diaper, and puts him back down, only to hear him cry again twenty minutes later. Karen heads down the hall, tripping again on the laundry and the talking toy, feeds and changes the baby and puts him back down . . . until it all starts again an hour later.

In this passage, we learned that:

a. Karen is stuck in the sequel to *Groundhog Day.*

b. Karen needs more sleep. Also, a laundry basket.

c. Karen's husband must be deaf in one ear or an extremely deep sleeper. Certainly, he isn't pretending not to hear that circus.

d. All of the above.

Sentence Completion

Choose the phrase that best completes the sentence.
Breast-feeding is:

a. All natural.

b. A good way to make your father turn beet red at family gatherings.

c. Easier said than done.

d. Quite a stunt to pull off when you have more babies than breasts.

Advanced Mathematics

Today, Eisha had to deal with three blowout diapers, five spit-ups, six clothing changes, two leaky breasts, and one migraine. How many times did Eisha get to sit down?

a. Three times, all on the toilet.
b. For one fleeting moment before the phone rang and the dog chased the cat out the door.
c. Does kneeling count?
d. Eisha can sleep standing up, like a horse or a zombie.

Science

Q. Which sentence best explains how gravity works?

a. After nursing three babies in four years, Susan's breasts no longer pointed forward, but downward toward a floor filled with colorful plastic toys.
b. Susan's ten-month-old loves to play Dropsies, so that by the end of a typical trip to Target she has retrieved toilet paper rolls, baby wipe refills, and greeting cards from among the aisles.
c. The dog frequently hangs out by the baby's high chair, waiting for Goldfish crackers and apple sauce to suddenly fall from above.
d. All of the above.

Chapter Two

The Baby Basics:

Sleeping, Eating, Pooping, and More

Everything You Want to Know About Babies
(But Are Too Tired to Ask)

When I was pregnant, a wise friend told me, "Everything you need to know about parenting babies, you'll learn in the first seventy-two hours." When it comes to the basics of diapering, swaddling, feeding, and soothing, this is mainly true. In fact, your hospital or health-care facility may even offer classes on breast-feeding and basic baby care. Or if you have a home birth, your doula can provide

Okay, I admit it. . . .

"It is okay not to do everything right. I spent so much time obsessing over getting everything right that I missed out on enjoying the time with my new baby."

—*Liz, Pompton Lakes, New Jersey*

Okay, I admit it. . . .

"I wish I would have known that the best way to fumble through the first months is trial and error."

—*Suz, Longwood, Florida*

you with this information. Still, if you are as clueless as I was about caring for babies, you might like to use this chapter as your cheat sheet.

Diapering 101

Whether you use cloth diapers or disposable ones, one thing is for sure: you're going to do a whole lotta diaper changing in those early weeks. In fact, the average newborn uses eight to ten diapers a day, even though she appears to eat far less than your husband, who likely doesn't poop as often. (I hope.)

Before you bring your baby home, set up at least one diaper changing station, most obviously at the baby's diaper changing table, and get all your gear, including the diaper pail, in easy reach. You should *never* leave your newborn on the changing table, not even for a second, no matter how immobile she appears to be. You just never know.

Keep the diapers stacked nearby, but place the baby oil and rash ointment out of reach of the baby, because one day, she's going to surprise you and figure out how to swat, grab, and/or hurl it. Put the wipes in a handy place, so you can flip open the container with one hand. I don't recommend wipe warmers, in part because the condensation often drips off the container and onto your changing table. Also, there's no sense in creating a Four Seasons–level of treatment for your baby when, eventually, you'll have to change her on the floor in a public place where you have no wipe warmer. (I know it sounds frighteningly harsh to you now in the glow of new motherhood, but you'll get there just like the rest of us. You'll see.)

I liked to keep a fresh diaper spread out and ready to slide under my baby's butt whenever possible. I also liked to pop open the diaper pail with my foot, but some of the newfangled pails don't make that easy. Test yours out without the baby nearby, and see what works for you. The bottom line is that you need to set up a system that makes it as easy as possible on you. Soon, you'll be able to change a diaper in your sleep. Literally.

If you have a boy, keep a burp cloth handy to place on his privates, or else you just might wind up with an unexpected shower. If you have a girl, make sure you carefully clean all the folds, and never wipe back to front, or you could transfer bacteria and cause a urinary infection.

I didn't use wipes on my newborns because they caused a terrible red rash on my firstborn, most likely from the chemicals in the wipes. Instead, I used cotton balls with water and/or baby oil until my babies were older. I've since found chlorine-free baby wipes at the health food store, but they cost a bit more than regular wipes. You can make your own wipes by soaking disposable or washable cloths in baby oil, which is simply mineral oil, and keeping them in a jar or an emptied and cleaned-out wipe container.

As for how to actually diaper a baby, with disposable diapers it's pretty easy. Just put the baby's bottom onto the opened diaper, making sure the back is face down. (It's the part without the cute

Okay, I admit it. . . .

"I wish someone had warned that I would be all-consumed with my baby's poop."

—*Leslie, Onarga, Illinois*

design.) Pull the front of the diaper through the baby's legs, and pull the peel-off covers off the fastening flaps. Then pull the diaper closed and tape the flaps to the front of the diaper so that it's tight enough to keep pee and poop in, but not so tight that your baby is uncomfortable.

Cloth diapers can be trickier, because you have to fold them in thirds before placing the baby on them. Then there's the issue of safety pins, though some diaper services offer cloth diapers with Velcro tabs. Diaper services also often supply containers for you to put soiled diapers in and never touch again, so look into that if you'd like to avoid dumping poop in the toilet.

"Whatever mistakes you make won't send your kid to therapy. Just relax and enjoy your time."

—*Rachel, Woodinville, Washington*

It worked for me!

Feeding Your Newborn

Even though my firstborn preferred to chug his bottles than to latch on to my breast, I stuck with pumping breast milk for a while. Breast-feeding my (full-term) second baby came much more easily, and so I nursed him for a few months before switching him to formula.

I'll bet I can find critics from both sides for anything and everything I did (and didn't do) when it came to feeding my newborn. So, I'm not about to tell you what to do. I think how you choose to feed your baby is a personal, private decision that's nobody's business but your own. And yet, I still get pangs of guilt. Go figure.

Here, I'll outline the basics of breast-feeding and bottle-feeding and leave it up to you to decide which way to go:

Breast-Feeding Basics

It's been ingrained in all parenting writers to start any discussion about feeding newborns with "breast milk is best." The Centers for Disease Control and Prevention reported in 2009 that nearly three-quarters of mothers nationwide try breastfeeding, though some states have higher rates. About 43 percent are still breastfeeding their babies at six months, though only 13 percent are breastfeeding exclusively. Many organizations, such as the American Academy of Pediatrics and the World Health Organization, encourage mothers to breastfeed their babies.

Here are some of the main cases for breast-feeding:

• Mother's milk contains at least 100 ingredients that formula doesn't have.

• Mother's milk has the right amount of fatty acids, lactose, water, and amino acids for your baby's digestion, brain development, and growth.

• Breast-fed babies have fewer illnesses, because the mother's milk transfers antibodies to the infant.

• Breast-feeding is less expensive than formula, and it's easier on the environment (no cans or bottles to create or recycle).

• Breast-feeding doesn't require that you clean bottles.

• Breast-feeding may reduce a mother's chances of getting breast cancer.

Getting Started

You'd think that something so natural would be easy to do. And for some mothers, it is. But for others, it takes some work. I highly recommend that you take advantage of breast-feeding classes offered while you're in the hospital, assuming that both you and the baby are healthy and able to attend. I was the only mother at breast-feeding classes without my firstborn, a preemie who was in the NICU, and frankly, it just served to remind me that I had bigger worries than how to breast-feed. Besides, the lactation specialist kept saying "irregardless," which is not a word and made me want to box her ears. What can I say? I was extremely hormonal.

If you plan to try breast-feeding, at least read up on it as much as you can *regardless* of whether you stick with it. Here's what you need to know about getting started with breast-feeding:

Okay, I admit it. . . .

"I wish I had really known what to expect, and how to make breast-feeding work well from the beginning. I assumed it would just come naturally, and although it does to some extent, there is so much that an experienced lactation specialist could have helped with."

—*Stacy, Forest Falls, California*

1. **Don't panic.** If your newborn doesn't latch on easily and starts to cry, try to stay calm, and ask a nurse, a lactation expert, or an experienced breast-feeder for help.

2. **Coax your baby's mouth open.** Once you've lined up his nose to your nipple, gently rub his mouth until it opens, and then stick your nipple into his mouth, which should cover most if not all of your areola (the darker skin around the nipple).

3. **Don't endure pain.** If it hurts, you're probably doing it wrong. Your baby might not latch on correctly, so check her mouth and make sure that it's covering the main part of your areola and that your nipple is pretty far back into your baby's mouth. If it does hurt, stick your finger into her mouth to break the seal, like you're releasing a suction cup from a window.

> **Okay, I admit it. . . .**
>
> "I was extremely emotional over not being able to breast-feed easily. I cried during so many feedings at the beginning; I just could not get over how unbelievably difficult and painful it was . . . for something that was meant to be so natural!"
>
> —*Sarah, Bloomington, Illinois*

4. **Keep trying until you find a comfortable position.** Some babies do best with the cradle hold, where you cradle your baby's head with the crook of your arm. Sometimes, though, you're better off using your opposite hand to hold

your baby's head, thereby creating more space for your breast and her head while she feeds. If you've had a C-section, you might want to try the football hold, where you hold the baby in the same-side arm as though you're going to head for a touchdown. Finally, you can nurse lying down with your baby on the bed next to you, but *be careful* that you don't fall asleep and roll over on your baby.

5. **Think twice before switching sides.** I was taught to switch breasts halfway through feeding, but there's increasing evidence that letting your baby finish on one breast before switching is best. The La Leche League and Dr. Sears are among the experts who say that it's important that your baby gets the fatty hindmilk that follows the initial foremilk (which is more like skim milk) when feeding. If your baby nurses on one breast only, or "finishes off" the first breast before switching, some experts believe this is perfectly okay. Just be sure to offer the other breast at the next feeding. You can help ease breast engorgement through pumping, though chances are, your body will adjust to your baby's breastfeeding style after a few days.

> "The more you supplement because baby 'isn't getting enough,' the more you'll damage your supply and doom your efforts. Trust your body and your baby!"
>
> —Heidi, St. Cloud, Florida

It worked for me!

"Find a buddy to talk about breast-feeding with. I didn't know it could be that easy until I saw a friend quickly and simply nurse her child. I was able to copy it, and now I've nursed two babies her way."

It worked for me!

—*Beth, Morris, Alabama*

6. **Feed frequently.** The American Academy of Pediatrics recommends that mothers nurse their babies eight to twelve times per twenty-four hours in the early weeks of the baby's life. You'll be able to figure out if your baby is hungry when she's more alert or active than usual, moving her mouth or "rooting," when she turns her head toward your breast, and sometimes, sticks her tongue out.

Nursing Know-How: Troubleshooting

As natural and wonderful as breast-feeding can be, sometimes it doesn't go all that smoothly, especially in the beginning when you're just getting the hang of it. Here are three typical breast-feeding issues and how to address them.

Sore nipples: If your baby isn't latching on right, you can wind up with sore nipples. The best treatment for sore nipples is prevention. In other words, learn how to breast-feed correctly early on, and you likely won't face this problem. Great advice, unless you're already "ouching" through nursing sessions.

A call to a lactation specialist, either through the hospital, your pediatrician, or a group like La Leche, can help you figure out the right way to nurse. Meanwhile, ask your ob-gyn for some safe nipple cream, such as lanolin oil.

Engorged breasts: This is when your breasts feel full, swollen, and a bit painful. In the early days of breast-feeding, your breasts can get engorged when your milk first comes in, and your body is adjusting to the flow. This is normal, and it'll get better in time. You can also often feel engorged when it's feeding time, but your baby isn't hungry or isn't with you. This is a great time to use a breast pump to release and save your milk for later.

Sometimes, though, breast engorgement is a more serious issue caused by a supply and demand problem that can actually make it harder for your baby to feed. If your areolas are flat, making it difficult for your newborn to feed, if the lymph nodes under your armpits are sore and swollen, or if you're running a fever of 100°F or more, call your doctor.

Leaking breasts: The good news is that leaking breasts will prevent engorgement. The bad news is that, chances are, you're going to discover your shirt is soaked with breast milk, probably at the coffee shop or in an equally embarrassing situation. Leaking generally stops after you've gotten the hang of breast-feeding, though some women are long-term leakers.

Until then, though, if you feel like your breasts are going to let down milk when you don't want them to, apply pressure to them using your crossed arms. If it's not time to feed your baby and you can get to your breast pump, use that to let a little bit of milk out and stop the leaking. Then invest in some good breast pads, preferably without plastic backings that can cause yeast infections. You might have to try a few before you find one that fits you well (and doesn't migrate out of your bra and onto the floor while you're in line at the bank).

> **It worked for me!**
>
> "Don't overpump or you'll end up with plugged ducts/mastitis, and you won't know why."
>
> —*Emily, San Jose, California*

Bottle-Feeding Basics

Whether you decide to supplement nursing with bottle-feeding your baby, breast-feed for just a few weeks or months, or skip breast-feeding altogether, you'll need to know what to expect from bottle-feeding. Here are the basics:

Get all the right gear. First, pick out a few different nipples. Your baby will decide which one she likes, and then you can stock up on those. They come in latex, silicone, and rubber and have varying opening sizes, which control how fast the formula or breast milk flow. Bear in mind that some environmental groups warn that latex and rubber nipples can cause allergic reactions, so ask your pediatrician before you choose.

Next, you'll need to choose a bottle. Plastic bottles aren't breakable but can deteriorate, especially

> **Okay, I admit it. . . .**
>
> "You are not a bad mom if the little one refuses to breast-feed. You have not failed her, and you will still be able to bond with her. Some babies just don't take to it. Let go of the guilt."
>
> —*Beckey, Steubenville, Ohio*

if you wash them in hot water in the dishwasher. Some experts believe that plastic bottles can leach dangerous levels of bisphenal-A (BPA), a synthetic hormone, into food. But manufacturers currently say there's no proof of harm to babies in more than thirty years of plastic bottle use. Nevertheless, BPA has been banned from baby bottles in Canada, and some U.S. states have banned their use in containers and cups used frequently by children. Glass bottles aren't known to have such issues, but handing an active baby or toddler a glass projectile isn't all that wise. Plastic liners, though, are said not to contain BPA. Whichever you choose, some experts recommend that you do not store milk in plastic bottles, which shouldn't be heated either in the microwave, electric bottle warmers, or in boiling water.

If you wander around Babies "R" Us, you'll find an entire aisle of baby bottle gear, but do you really need all that stuff? Minimally, you'll need some sort of bottle holder/cooler for when you're on the go. No doubt you'll get some when you're in the hospital, but you might want to invest in something stronger (and more stylish). You can buy bottle warmers, but given the new concerns over chemicals in plastic, you might want to reconsider. I had terrific bottles that stored powdered formula in a bubble of sorts at the base. Then I'd flip up the nipple, releasing the formula into water. No need to warm anything up, and it cut down on (stinky) leaking formula while we were out.

You might want to get a drying rack for bottles, and you should certainly stock up on burp clothes, whether you're bottle- or breast-feeding. I got lucky: my mother-in-law sewed some for me. But you can get some at any baby supply store, or just use soft towels or cloth diapers—anything but your shirt, unless you're super desperate.

Choose an infant formula. If you're not bottle-feeding with your own breast milk, you'll need to pick out a formula. There are so many different formulas, all with different, well, formulas, some involving cow's milk protein, others soy, and many fortified with vitamins. Then there are those that are specially created for babies who have digestive issues, such as reflux or colic. These are especially costly, but your pediatrician may recommend them if your baby is having trouble keeping traditional formula down. Some formulas are fortified with DHA and ARA, nutrients that some doctors say are found naturally in breast milk. There's been some controversy surrounding these ingredients regarding adverse reactions. Be sure to Google all ingredients in formula to find out the latest research before you choose an infant formula for your child. And remember, babies under one year should not drink cow's milk.

Okay, I admit it. . . .

"I struggled with the breast-feeding versus bottle-feeding issue . . . and finally a trusted friend said to me: 'You are feeding your baby. Don't let anyone give you a hard time.' It meant a lot to me."

—*Kris, Clarkfield, Minnesota*

Feed on demand. Most experts these days say you should feed your baby on demand. In the beginning, that'll likely be every two to three hours. To me, three hours would have felt like an entire day when my preemie was busy catching up to bigger babies by eating all the time. Until your newborn hits ten pounds, she'll probably drink between one and three ounces of formula at each feeding. Make sure you keep the bottle at a forty-five-degree angle, so your newborn doesn't get extra air. *Never* prop the bottle and leave your baby alone with it, because she could choke. Make sure you burp her after she eats a few ounces to release any built-up air.

Catching Zzzz's

I'll go more into detail about getting your baby to sleep in Chapter 5, but I thought I'd round off this chapter by giving you some basics about the very thing that may seem elusive to you in the beginning weeks or months: meaningful, restorative sleep. Unless you're lucky enough to get a baby who sleeps through the night from the beginning, you're in for a fair to goodly amount of sleep deprivation that could take its toll on you. But there are some things you can do from the start to help your newborn sleep better, sooner.

First, understand that though newborns sleep upward of fourteen to eighteen hours a day during the first week, leveling off to about twelve to sixteen hours a day after about a month, they rarely sleep more than two to four hours at a clip. And neither will you. Some babies hit a long stretch of sleep by two months, but most don't get there until they are five or six months old. So be

Okay, I admit it. . . .

"I wish someone would have told me it's a good idea to have at least a month's supply of everything needed for the baby on hand. They sure go through diapers and formula quicker than you realize."

—*Lisa, Patton, Pennsylvania*

prepared for many sleepless nights ahead.

Still, you can help foster your newborn's sleep in these ways:

Start a bedtime routine. In the beginning, bedtime should simply involve a diaper change, feeding, and a lullaby. Anything more involved than that (save reading for when she's older) will pretty much ensure a complicated and long bedtime routine come toddlerhood and beyond, likely involving pleading and perhaps bribery. Don't go there.

Teach him the difference between night and day. For the first few days, there's really nothing you can do about your newborn's whacked-out schedule. But after about two weeks, you can start to teach your newborn that there's a difference between night and day (beyond the sun going down and your feeling extra dog tired, that is.) During daylight hours, keep lights on, make plenty of noise, and interact with your newborn often. At night, though, talk in hushed tones, turn down the lights, and don't interact with him as much.

Okay, I admit it. . . .

"I was scared to death and couldn't believe those people at the hospital let me take this tiny, helpless baby home with me when I obviously had no idea what I was doing!"

—*Danielle, Greentown, Indiana*

It worked for me!

"Take it hour by hour, and don't count the minutes till your husband returns. Just think, 'What can I do in this minute for the baby, and for myself?' and do it."

—*Beth, Morris, Alabama*

Gimme a break

Be a little selfish

Don't be afraid to be a little bit selfish with your time, your house, and your newborn. If you're not up to having visitors, simply say as politely as possible that next week would be a better time for a visit. If that's not your style, tell folks that your pediatrician has suggested that you keep the baby away from other people for X amount of time. Remember, as wonderful as it is to welcome a baby into the world, it can also be exhausting and overwhelming. You need to make your life easier, not harder, so that you can best care for your newborn—and yourself.

Okay, I admit it. . . .

"Bringing another life into this world really put things in perspective for me; my priorities shifted 180 degrees. I became a better person. Of course, being able to cuddle and snuggle the little wee one and have them look to you as if you are the greatest thing ever is quite satisfying too."

— *Michele, Atlanta, Georgia*

New Mom Mad Libs:
The Lullaby

Hush, little baby, don't say a word,
Momma's gonna buy you a Soothing Sounds White Noise Machine.

And if that Soothing Sounds White Noise Machine won't work,
Momma's gonna buy you a Dream Time Automatic Cradle Rocker.

And if that Dream Time Automatic Cradle Rocker proves useless,
Momma's gonna buy you a DVD of a J-Lo movie.

And if that J-Lo movie doesn't make you snooze,
Momma's gonna buy you a plane ticket to Grandma's.

And if Grandma doesn't get you to sleep,
Momma's gonna buy you a room at a local sleep clinic.

And if that sleep clinic doesn't fix it,
Momma's gonna hire you a night nurse named Rachel the Ruthless.

And if that Rachel the Ruthless won't bring back sleep time,
Momma's gonna buy you a professional grade soundproof wall.

And if that professional grade soundproof wall fails,
Momma's gonna go wake up Daddy with a bullhorn.

Chapter Three

Month by Month:
So Many Milestones, So Little Time

Crawling and Eating and Walking, Oh My!

Baby's first year is so filled with milestones, and there are numerous calendars, journals, and even wall charts out there to keep track of them. And you will. You'll see. You'll also call Grandma when Baby rolls over for the first time, and possibly even post the exciting exclusive world premiere video on YouTube. This is because (a) you're proud of your child for accomplishing something more than filling diapers, and (b) newborns are boring. But babies, well, they are something else entirely—

Okay, I admit it. . . .

"It makes my heart jump to watch him roll over for the first time, try to crawl, and turn himself 360 degrees!"

—*Keren, Grand Forks, North Dakota*

39

Okay, I admit it. . . .

"My favorite thing is seeing my baby's firsts—first smiles, first laughs, first sounds. As soon as he smiled at me the first time, it wiped away all the exhaustion and overwhelming feeling that I wouldn't be a good parent."

—*Cindy, Hillsdale, New Jersey*

something that's going to take up to four gigabytes of disk space on your video camera, and then some.

It's pretty amazing if you think about it: your baby starts the year as not much more than an eating, sleeping (if you're lucky), and pooping machine, and ends it crawling, maybe even walking, saying a word or two, and having his very own little personality. From rolling over to gumming his very first Cheerio, the first year is one cause for celebration after another. So charge your camera's batteries and get ready. The fun is about to begin!

Great Expectations and the Strong Urge to Compare

Before I get to the milestones, I need to say a word about comparing your baby to other babies: don't. Babyhood isn't a competition, and even if your baby is the first to walk, it doesn't make you Mother of the Year. Nor does it guarantee your kid a spot on the New England Patriots or the U.S. Olympic track team. It just means she walked first. Yay for you.

If, on the other hand, your baby seems to lag way behind other babies, do take note of it. Call your pediatrician if you have concerns that your baby isn't reaching milestones in a reasonable (read: *not* merely a few days late) amount of time.

Also, remember that if your baby was a preemie, she'll likely hit milestones later than other babies. My preemie pretty much did everything five weeks late as he was born five weeks early.

So what will your baby be able to do and when? Here's the scoop:

Month One: Small Milestones, Big Deal

By one month old, *most* babies can:

• Respond to sounds

• Lift their heads while lying on their stomachs

• Stare at your face or objects that are about six inches away

By one month old, *about half* of all babies can:

• Follow objects with their eyes

• Say baby sounds like ooh and aah (perfect for future fireworks watching)

• See black-and-white patterns (which is why those black-and-white mobiles are so popular; remember, though, babies can see only about six inches from their faces, and mobiles should be hung out of reach)

By one month old, *a few advanced* babies can:

• Smile

• Laugh

• Hold up their heads at a forty-five-degree angle

(But don't get out the Harvard application just yet. Babies reach every milestone at varying schedules.)

Month Two: More Humanlike

By two months old, *most* babies can:

• Vocalize ("goo" and gurgling)

• Follow objects with their eyes

• Notice their hands ("Hey! What are these things that are always here?")

• Hold up their heads for short amounts of time

By two months old, *about half* of all babies can:

• Smile

• Laugh

• Hold up their heads at a forty-five-degree angle

• Move more smoothly (and less like Jeff Bridges's rigid alien-in-a-human body character from *Star Man*)

By two months old, *some advanced* babies can:

• Hold their heads steady

• Bear weight on their legs (and "stand" in your lap when you hold them)

• Lift their heads while on their bellies

Month Three: Getting to Know You

By three months old, *most* babies can:

• Recognize Mommy's face

• Hold their heads steady

• Track moving objects with their eyes (like big sister, a toy, or the dog)

By three months old, *about half* of all babies can:

• Vocalize by gurgling and cooing

• Blow bubbles (spit, not Bazooka)

• Recognize Mommy's voice

• Push up on their arms while on their bellies (like a little modified push-up)

By three months old, *some advanced* babies can:

• Roll over (thereby changing diaper-changing time)

• Turn toward loud sounds

• Bring their hands together and whack their hands at various objects

WE ASKED: What's your favorite thing about the baby days?

"Watching all the firsts—first smile, first time he rolled over, first time he grabbed my finger."

—Jennifer, Oconomowoc, Wisconsin

WE ASKED: Did you worry about your baby reaching milestones at the right time?

Constantly: 14%
Now and then: 42%
Seldom: 28%
Never: 16%

Month Four: Not a Newborn Anymore

By four months old, *most* babies can:

• Smile

• Laugh

• Bear weight on their legs

• Coo when you talk to them

By four months old, *about half* of all babies can:

• Grasp a toy (also your finger, glasses, keys . . . be careful)

• Roll over

By four months old, *advanced* babies can:

• Imitate sounds (like "dada," though you're hoping for "mama")

• Get their first tooth

• Be ready for solids (Check with your pediatrician before starting solids.)

Month Five: Getting Ready to Sit Up

By five months old, *most* babies can:

• See bold colors

• Play with their feet and hands (conveniently located toys you never leave in the shopping cart)

By five months old, *about half* of all babies can:

• Recognize their own names

• Turn toward sounds

• Roll over in both directions

By five months old, *advanced* babies can:

• Sit without support for a moment or two (Get ready to catch her head on its way down.)

• Gum or mouth objects

Month Six: Loads of Baby Fun

By six months old, *most* babies can:

• Turn toward sounds

• Imitate sounds

• Roll over in both directions

By six months old, *about half* of all babies can:

• Start solid foods (Again, check with the doc.)

- Sit without help or support

- Gum or mouth objects

- Pass toys and other objects from one hand to the other

By six months old, *advanced* babies can:

- Attempt to crawl (At first, it might be a lunge in one direction without the full-out crawling.)

- Use more than one sound to create "baby talk" (It sounds like a language from a *Star Wars* extra, but really, it's just gibberish.)

- Drag themselves along the floor

Okay, I admit it. . . .

"Every child is different! Really—everyone says it, but it's true! My first walked at nine months, and my last walked at sixteen months."

—*Jenny, Paulsbo, Washington*

WE ASKED: How did you help your baby learn to walk?

"All four did it on their own. They had to walk to keep up with the big people."

—*Kellie, Red Deer, Washington*

Month Seven: The Social Butterfly

By seven months old, *most* babies can:

- Sit without help or support

- Drag themselves along the floor or toward an object (Cats, beware.)

By seven months old, *about half* of all babies can:

• Crawl (Warning: I found out the hard way that my baby could crawl under the couch.)

• Jabber ("talk")

• Experience shyness or anxiety around strangers

By seven months old, *advanced* babies can:

• Wave bye-bye

• Stand while holding on to something (But spot them, because you never know when their legs will give out.)

• Bang things together (lucky you)

• Understand that people and things are still there even if they can't see them (i.e., your head has not disappeared during peekaboo, after all)

Month Eight: Chatterbox

By eight months old, *most* babies can:

• Say "mama" and/or "dada," though they might attribute them to the wrong people (i.e., all men are "dada" or even "mama")

• Pass toys and other objects from one hand to the other

By eight months old, *about half* of all babies can:

• Stand while holding on to something

- Crawl

- Point at things

- Look for things

By eight months old, *advanced* babies can:

- Pull themselves up to stand

- "Cruise" (move along while holding furniture, toys, your legs, etc.)

- Drink from a sippy cup (Most moms I know keep the bottle until one year; breast-feeding moms might add additional fluids in a sippy cup around now.)

- Pick things up with a finger and a thumb

- Gesture that they want something (ball, bottle, toy, that expensive bowl full of candies at Grandma's . . .)

> **It worked for me!**
>
> I helped him to stand and would practice with him a little each day, until one day around nine months he just started pulling himself up at the sofa."
>
> —*Rachel, Bensalem, Pennsylvania*

Month Nine: Now We're Cruising

By nine months old, *most* babies can:

- Stand while holding on to something

- Jabber or combine syllables

• Understand that people and things are still there even if they can't see them

By nine months old, *about half* of all babies can:

• Cruise

• Drink from a sippy cup

• Eat with their hands

• Bang objects together

By nine months old, *advanced* babies can:

• Play games like peekaboo and patty-cake

• Say "mama" and "dada" and actually get it right

Month Ten: Starts to Stand

By ten months old, *most* babies can:

• Wave bye-bye

• Pick things up with one finger and a thumb

• Crawl, even with belly off the ground (thereby making them faster and harder to catch)

By ten months old, *about half* of all babies can:

• Say "mama" and "dada" and actually get it right

• Gesture toward things they want

By ten months old, *advanced* babies can:

• Stand alone without help for a few seconds (while you hold your breath)

• Put things into containers (Tip: Look for your phone in the diaper pail.)

It worked for me!

"After she started showing signs of her readiness to walk, my husband and I would play a game of 'pass the baby' each night. We'd sit across from each other and pass the baby back and forth. Before you knew it, she was taking her own steps to each of us!"

—*Kathy, Sykesville, Maryland*

Month Eleven: And We're Off!

By eleven months old, *most* babies can:

• Imitate other people's actions

• Gesture toward things they want

Okay, I admit it. . . .

"We let her cruise on the furniture and holding her hands whenever possible, but really let her take her time. We have a fifty-pound dog, so that impeded her progress a bit."

—*Sarah, Kindsbach, New Jersey*

By eleven months old, *about half* of all babies can:

• Take a few steps (Again, spot them!)

• Say another word besides "mama" and "dada" (Ours were "ball" and "wheel" here.)

By eleven months old, *advanced* babies can:

- Take a few steps without help (One son could; my other son took another month.)

- Scribble (Store those crayons up high.)

- Say one word besides "mama" and "dada"

Okay, I admit it. . . .

"I talked to him *constantly* ... even in public. Problem is, now that he's in school, I *still* talk to myself in the supermarket, 'Should we get this cereal?' People look at me funny."

—*Denise, Belleville, New Jersey*

Month Twelve: The Finish Line

By twelve months old, *most* babies can:

- Imitate other people's actions (blow kisses, wave bye-bye, generally act like Miss America on a float at the Rose Bowl parade)

- Recognize family members in photos and in person

By twelve months old, *about half* of all babies can:

- Take a few steps without help

- Say one word besides "mama" and "dada"

- Understands many words

- Shake their heads "no" (thereby officially kicking off toddlerhood)

By twelve months old, *advanced* babies can:

- Walk all by themselves (Yay, for your back; boo, for your legs.)

- Say two words besides "mama" and "dada"

> "Whatever I did, I explained to my baby: 'I am changing your diaper. I am washing your hair. I am counting your toes. I love you,' and so on."
>
> —*Marilyn, Bensalem, Pennsylvania*

It worked for me!

Phew! That's a lot of milestones in a short period of time. Think about it: If adults attempted to do something entirely new as often as babies do, we'd need more time lying on the couch watching Tivoed episodes of *Mad Men* to get over it all.

Yet babies can get fussy right before a major milestone. Sometimes, they drool and may even run a little temperature before they teethe. They might lose sleep just before they're ready to crawl or walk, and they babble a lot before they manage to get out their first words. Take note of changes in their behavior, as it just might precede a milestone. Do you know where the video camera is?

What If My Baby Is Behind?

Chances are, your pediatrician will catch any developmental delays at your baby's well visits. But I wouldn't leave it all in his or her hands. You're with your baby far longer than the twenty-minute doctor's visit, so you know better whether your baby has or hasn't reached his milestones. Don't be afraid to mention any concerns you have to the doctor. Follow your gut if you feel something is wrong.

But please, don't obsess over milestones. Babies change so very quickly that a missed milestone might be reached in a few weeks, days, or even hours. Keep a watchful eye, but don't stand at the ready with your baby's milestone book, waiting to record his next move. Compare his activity to other kids, but only as a loose gauge. Just because your baby misses a milestone one month doesn't necessarily mean it's cause for alarm. (And conversely, just because your kid hits the mark ahead of all the other babies at Mommy & Me class doesn't make him the next Einstein either. In fact, Einstein was a late talker.)

Remember, every kid is different, and so they achieve milestones differently. This chapter simply provides guidelines for averages, so you have an idea of what your baby should be able to do and when.

> "Just be patient and continue to read, talk, sing, play, whatever with your baby and know that each step will be achieved when your child is ready."
>
> —*Suz, Longwood, Florida*

It worked for me!

"No two snowflakes are alike, and neither are any two babies. Forget what your friends in the moms group are saying about their babies' accomplishments. (They are probably stretching the truth.) If you are going to the recommended doctor's appointments, your pediatrician will pick up on any issues."

It worked for me!

—*Alice, Sugar Land, Texas*

Gimme a break

Mom Has Milestones, Too

In this age of the crazed Supermom, you, too, will have milestones—only they're more about not doing things than doing things. Once you learn to let go of the idea of perfection, you'll settle into a more manageable motherhood that's healthier for you and your family. Keep an eye out for these milestones of your very own:

1. You give up on trying to keep a perfect house.
2. You stop trying to create the perfect baby.
3. You stop comparing yourself to other mothers.
4. You realize that nobody's perfect.

Some moms figure this all out in the first year. Others take longer, and still others never get it. The sooner you forget trying to be Supermom, the better.

Just a minute!

Baby Milestone Charts
(According to the Moms in Your Playgroup)

Age	Milestone
1 month	Sleeps through the night, awakening only after Mommy has showered, mopped the kitchen floor, and finished sending the last of 500 baby announcements
2 months	Holds up head, smiles, laughs, and generally acts like the host of a popular talk show
3 months	Pushes up onto his hands while lying on belly, and adds a clap between push-ups, like Sylvester Stallone in Rocky 4
4 months	Rolls over, retrieves lost items from under the couch, and then sorts them into bins from The Container Store
5 months	Sits without support (unless you count two chairs and a huge, strategically placed pillow as "support")
6 months	Uses baby talk to complement fluency in sign language (also, Mandarin Chinese)
7 months	Waves bye-bye and even throws in a kiss and a wink for Grandma, unprompted
8 months	Crawls (faster than anybody else's baby)

9 months	Cruises the furniture, dusting and straightening up the breakables along the way
10 months	Walks, and not all clunky like Frankenstein, either
11 months	Runs the 100-yard dash
12 months	Talks, mostly about the economy and sailing

Chapter Four

Things People Might Not Tell You
About Babies and Motherhood

W hen I think about it now, I'm embarrassed, yet also amused. I actually recorded onto a legal pad every single feeding and bowel movement my firstborn made—and then showed it to the pediatrician. Luckily, he was kind enough to pretend to look at it and not burst into giggles. Certainly, he didn't need to know the consistency of every single one of my newborn's poops for a week. But I was a nervous new mom with a preemie, and I wanted to make sure I wasn't missing anything important.

Okay, I admit it. . . .

"I wish someone had told me that newborns make all kinds of noises and that they are normal. Don't freak out over twitches and snorts of air."

—*Michele, Atlanta, Georgia*

My Poop Log was only the first of my attempts to ease my own confusion over motherhood. There was so much to take in, and so few awake and alert brain cells to process it all. I could run some of my issues by the pediatrician, but not all of them. After all, what do you tell the nurse who answers the phone when you want to know how to get your newly crawling baby out from under the couch? Some things are best learned on your own. Others, though, require some assistance from moms who've been through the very same thing.

In this chapter, I'll cover some of the things you might be confused about, as well as some of those things nobody tells you about. Even if you're busy making your own Poop Log, it just may help with what's confusing you today.

 WE ASKED: What do you wish someone had told you about parenting a baby?

"That it would take you an extra hour to get ready to go anywhere, and just as you were ready to walk out the door baby decides to soil her diaper or gets hungry."

—*Ashley, Hamilton, Oklahoma*

"I wish someone had told me to go by my instincts as a mother and not what I thought was the right thing to do."

—*Heidi, St. Cloud, Florida*

Getting a Gut Check

The famed Dr. Benjamin Spock began his classic 1946 parenting book *The Common Sense Book of Baby and Child Care* with words that still hold true: "You know more than you think you do." Only, when Dr. Spock published his book, parenting was much simpler. Remember, this was long before we were expected to play Beethoven for our babies in utero and baby-proof the oven door. (Go check. I'll wait.)

Yet it still makes sense to follow your instincts whenever possible. Then add in a few go-to sources, such as other moms, chat rooms, and this book, to help you make your parenting decisions. A gut check—in moderation—never hurts. Here are a few things you may wonder about.

#1: The Smallest Person in the House Requires the Most Stuff

My husband and I were overwhelmed by the aisles and aisles of baby stuff we encountered when we went to sign up for our baby registry. "Do we really need all this stuff?" I mumbled, while he disappeared behind the mountain of Pack 'n Plays. "God, I hope not," I answered my own question. And yet, there we were a year later, packing for a family trip to the beach with so much stuff in and on top of our SUV we looked like the Clampetts rolling into Beverly Hills.

You really do need a lot of the stuff you'll add to your baby registry, but not all of it. Certainly, you should stock up on diapers—but not so many that your baby outgrows them before she uses them all up. I wouldn't buy too many wipes at once until you figure out which brand works best for your baby. Same goes for lotions and shampoos. Here are the most essential of baby essentials:

- Diapers

- Wipes (Only use after one month old, or they could cause a rash.)

- Diaper rash cream

- Diaper pail

- Bibs

- baby oil, lotions, shampoo (If you're lucky, someone gave you a basket of this stuff at your shower. Don't buy more until you pick a brand you like.)

- Burp clothes

- Blankets for swaddling

- Onesies

- Clothes, socks, hats, snowsuits (My friend got something like a dozen snowsuits at her shower. Really, you just need two so that you have a spare in case of spit-up, spilled bottles, etc.)

- Infant car seat and, for later, a regular car seat

- Diaper bag

- Bottles if you're bottle-feeding

- Breast pump (I preferred the double electronic kind.)

- Baby nail clippers (Practice!)

- Baby thermometer

- Pacifiers (Unless you're against them on principal, get a bunch of them. They tend to disappear when you need them the most.)

- Bassinet and/or crib

- Rocking chair or glider

- Hooded bath towels

- Stroller

And those are just the basics. Now, here are a few things that you don't necessarily need, but if you really want them (or Grandma wants something to do at Babies "R" Us), go right ahead and get them:

"As hard as it is to resist, don't buy a lot of clothes. Babies grow very quickly. There's always another cute outfit in another store."

It worked for me!

—Angela, Corpus Christi, Texas

- Baby bathtub (It can be handy at first, but babies outgrow them fast, and then you wind up bathing them in the bathtub anyhow. The sink works fine, too.)

- Spoons, bowls, and other feeding supplies (He won't need them for about six months.)

- High chair (Why have it clogging up kitchen space when you won't need it for at least six months—unless someone else wants to spring for it. In that case, take it.)

- Childproofing stuff (I'd go ahead and get the electrical outlet covers, but other than that, you won't really need the doorway gates or the cabinet locks right away. And don't waste your money on too many gadgets, such as the toilet lid latch my kids broke into like Houdini. See what's working for your friends with kids a little older than yours and read online reviews before you buy childproofing gear.)

- Playmat (A blanket works just fine, too, but some of those playmats do come with fun stuff that hangs just within baby's reach—up to you.)

- Pack 'n Play (We used ours as a portable crib for trips. Other than that, nobody really sticks their babies in a playpen these days.)

- Baby swing (It does come in handy if you'd like to prepare lunch with both hands. Some folks swear by them. Personally, we preferred the doorway jumper.)

- Baby monitor (If your house is big, get one. We had a video one, which really wasn't necessary, except when my older son started climbing out of his crib—relax; you've got time.)

• Wipe warmers (The condensation gets all over everything. Plus, baby then gets used to warm wipes, which you won't have with you in the chilly bathroom at the mall.)

WE ASKED: What must-carry items are always in your diaper bag?

"Diapers, butt cream, snacks, extra dry clothes, spare keys for car, change for coffee."

—Kellie, Red Deer, Washington

"Plastic disposable bags for yucky diapers, yucky clothes, dirty toys."

—Kellie, Derby, Connecticut

#2: You May Not Fall Completely, Madly in Love with Your Newborn

With all those celebrity magazines out there showing pictures of blissful new moms under headlines like "Baby Lust!" it's hard to believe that you might not feel totally in love with your baby right away or all the time. Think about it: if your husband had kept you up all night with his crying and fussing when you were dating, how would that relationship have turned out? Or maybe you've got a baby who sleeps all the time and doesn't do much else. It's hard to bond with someone who's always snoring at you. And guess what? That's okay. It's okay to feel tired or a bit overwhelmed at times. It's even okay to dream of those pre-baby days when you could just dash out of the house whenever you felt like hitting Starbucks for

Okay, I admit it. . . .

"I thought there was something wrong with my baby because he slept all the time."

—*Danielle, Greentown, Indiana*

a latte and some long, leisurely newspaper reading. (Note: If you continue to feel detached or even violent toward your baby, though, seek help. It could be a sign of postpartum depression or psychosis.)

#3: Breast-Feeding Can Take Work

I know breast-feeding looks natural and easy, but for some women, it requires some practice and some patience. Others don't get the hang of it at all, or choose not to try. Frankly, what you decide to do about breast-feeding is your business. Sometimes though, other people won't treat it that way. If you decide to give it a go, make sure you arm yourself with the resources to help you get through any rough spots, including the phone number of a lactation specialist; pamphlets, books, and websites on breast-feeding; and a friend who overcame some of her own nursing issues. These might include: cracked nipples, a baby who won't latch on, painful breast-feeding, not producing enough milk, or multiple babies to feed at once.

Okay, I admit it. . . .

"My second child had colic for three months, then an ear infection, and then he teethed. I swear he was four months old before I really liked him!"

—*Danielle, Franklin, Ohio*

Try to take it a day or even an hour at a time, because the hardest part of nursing often happens in the first few weeks. If you can make it through the early days, remember that it usually gets easier soon thereafter. If, however, you decide to switch to bottle-feeding, remind yourself that there are people who will take issue with that, but that's their problem, not yours. There's always someone who nursed longer than you did, or nursed exclusively. Remember, only you know what's right for you and your baby.

Okay, I admit it. . . .

"I wish I knew that the baby shouldn't need to nurse for seven hours straight the first two nights at home. It turned out that I had a legitimate problem with my milk supply, but I didn't realize it."

—*Pam, Urbandale, Iowa*

It worked for me!

"Breastfeeding is a commitment. It takes a long time for you and your baby to get into the groove of things."

—*Laura, Dyer, Indiana*

#4: Revise, Revamp and/or Abandon Your Plans to Fit Your Baby's Needs

Before you had a baby, you probably had grand plans for how everything would go once you got home from the hospital. You read up on how to introduce the dog to the new baby. You organized the baby's room. You picked out baby announcements. And then the dog hid behind the couch for two days, the baby threw up

Okay, I admit it. . . .

"The worst part of having a baby is suddenly realizing that you really don't know what the future will hold, and that you really don't have total control over it."

—*Kathy, Sykesville, Maryland*

all over the dressing table, and the girl you thought you were having turned out to be a boy— a boy who probably won't like his pink bedroom when he gets older.

Welcome to motherhood. Sometimes it goes as smoothly as a commercial for baby powder. Other times, not so much. That's when it's controlled chaos— or just plain chaos. The more rigid you are, the harder mothering may be at times, because babies don't always go along with the plan. One minute you're setting out for a nice walk with the baby in the stroller, and the next you're back in the house trying to figure out why the baby is wailing. One day you're bringing home size one diapers, and the next day, the baby needs a size two. Learn to revise your plans quickly, and you'll feel more comfortable in motherhood.

It worked for me!

"It's okay if you bought a beautiful crib, but your baby sleeps best on your chest in the recliner. Just go with the flow!"

—*Angie, Washburn, Missouri*

#5: Grandma Really Does Know What She's Talking About—Most of the Time

Forget for a moment that your mother used to put you in a basket on the floor of her car when you were a baby. Also, try to overlook that she put you to sleep on your tummy, fed you cereal in your bottle, and committed other travesties of old-fashioned parenting. Grandma actually does know how to take care of your baby.

Today's moms tend to act like we've invented motherhood. Granted, we have higher standards than our mothers did when it comes to safety. They didn't even have "Baby on Board" signs back in the day! Or proper car seats. Or outlet covers. Or did they? I don't even remember. I do remember, though, that I never wore a seatbelt until New Jersey passed a state law requiring it the same year I got my driver's license.

Times have changed, but baby care basics really haven't. Sure, we have newfangled wipe warmers, sleek strollers, and video baby monitors with better resolution than the black-and-white TV sets of yore. But the troika of babydom—eating, sleeping, pooping—remains the same.

Okay, I admit it. . . .

"My grandmother, bless her heart, constantly told me, 'Well, when I had my boys . . .' followed by what she did that is very much opposite of what the AAP recommends, such as letting them sleep on their tummies; feeding them at one month old; giving them milk, honey, nuts, and so on. I learned that whatever she told me, I should go ask my mom, but usually do the opposite."

—*Kristen, Modesto, California*

Okay, I admit it. . . .

"I was worried that I would make all the same mistakes my mother made. I have a wonderful mom, but no one is perfect. I am making different mistakes. I think that the mistakes mothers make might actually help build character in both the mother and child."

—*Andrea, Meriden, New Hampshire*

When you let your parents or in-laws take care of your baby, demand a few must-do rules, such as using the car seat properly and banning honey before age one. After all, you've got science on your side. Otherwise, let them care for your baby in their own way, even if it means that your baby is going to wear socks when she doesn't need them. The grandparents can do it—really!

#6: Daddy Isn't Going to Have the Same Experience as You

You're both the parents of the same baby, and yet, it appears that the father of your child doesn't exactly feel or act the same way you do. Sometimes, it may confound you that he has no clue how to pack a diaper bag, or perhaps that he's a far better diaperer, and yet he can't find the baby lotion. Maybe he's all about play, play, play, while you're about setting up the baby's pediatrician appointment and washing onesies. Or perhaps he's the night owl who loves to get up with the baby (you lucky duck), while you can barely keep your eyes open past 9:00 PM.

I've witnessed too many mothers, especially new ones, dismiss their husbands as useless clods who just don't understand how to do anything right. It's as though they expect the fathers to mother. But there are several reasons why they might not be able or willing to do exactly as you say.

Okay, I admit it. . . .

"Being a parent is a different experience for everyone."

—*Suz, Longwood, Florida*

First, they're not going through the hormone-induced emotional roller coaster that you may experience after giving birth. Even women who've adopted have said they've felt those same ups and downs while the men generally don't.

Second, chances are you're the primary caregiver, so your learning curve is shorter simply because you spend more time with the baby. And then when Hubby does try to help out, perhaps you criticize him until it's not even worth it for him to try.

Finally, he's not you. And just like he probably doesn't drive or eat or watch TV the same way you do, it's likely he won't parent like you. The sooner you let him be the daddy he wants to be, the better for everyone—unless, of course, the baby's safety is at issue. Then you've got to step in. Also, if he decides he really does want to be a useless clod and do nothing, then you've got to demand that he man up and help out, because chances are, there are two parents of your baby who should both be in on the parenting gig.

Okay, I admit it. . . .

"I wish someone had beaten it into my head with a stick that most of what the baby is doesn't depend completely on me. I felt responsible for *everything*—even things that had nothing to do with me as a mom."

—*Carrie, Louisville, Kentucky*

#7: You Might Be Tired Like You've Never Been Tired Before

Take the effects of a few all-nighters in college, combine them with the stress of a new job that has little oversight and few breaks, and add a dash of hormonal upheaval, and you'll begin to understand what baby-induced sleep deprivation will feel like. Maybe you're already there. (If so, close your eyes and take a snooze right now. I'll be here when you get up.)

If you're one of the lucky few whose babies sleep through the night from the beginning, skip ahead. (We're going to talk about you.) Now, unlike the ridiculously fortunate parents who've skipped ahead to the next section, most parents experience copious amounts of sleeplessness. And other people—especially parents who are currently well-rested—will tease you about it, making it sound like it's really no big deal. But it is.

There's a reason that sleep deprivation is a form of torture: It can break you down both physically and emotionally. It can also make you do silly things, like buy eight containers of parmesan cheese one shopping trip at a time—because I was so tired I forgot I'd already done it. (For baby number two, it was chili powder.) It can also be dangerous, affecting your ability to drive safely, for example.

Okay, I admit it. . . .

"I was extremely tired and grumpy due to the hormones and lack of sleep."

—*Danielle, Franklin, Ohio*

If you're tired like you've never been tired before, find ways to get that much-needed, coveted sleep. It sounds like a cliché, but sleep when the baby sleeps. Don't be afraid to ask a friend or family member to watch the baby, so you can get some shut-eye. You need it—and your baby needs you to get it. (The parmesan cheese is optional.)

#8: Hormones Rule

This topic actually goes hand-in-hand with the bit about sleep deprivation. Your postpartum hormones will send you to places you've never been before. From the commercial for Feed the Children that leaves you sobbing in the middle of *Oprah*, to the shampoo top your husband forgot to screw back on which sends you into a tizzy about "respect" or the lack thereof, you may feel as though your emotions have been hijacked. And guess what? They have.

I mentioned before that your postpartum hormones can be all over the place, making you a jumbled mess of emotions. Add sleep deprivation and dripping breasts, stitches in unmentionable areas, and what may feel like the world's largest muffin top, and it's no wonder you're all weepy.

Most of the time, it's manageable, like a bad case of PMS. Other times, though, it's much more serious. If your baby blues can't be fixed by a good cry and a nap,

Okay, I admit it. . . .

"Sleep when they sleep. When my baby slept, I caught up on household work. If your husband/partner works, you will be the one getting up all through the night. Your body needs sleep to maintain a steady stress level."

—*Paula, Worth, Illinois*

Okay, I admit it. . . .

"I wish I had realized just how hormonal I would be and that it's okay to tell family members to leave or what they can do to be helpful, even in-laws."

—*Andrea, Meriden, New Hampshire*

Okay, I admit it. . . .

"No one warned me about how sleep deprived I would be or that the first week baby blues were the worst. I'd cry over nothing at the drop of a hat!"

—*Jennifer, Aurora, Colorado*

persisting for weeks, rather than days, call your ob-gyn. And if you think you might harm yourself or the baby, seek immediate help. Postpartum depression can be hush-hush in some circles, but it's actually very common— and very treatable. Allow yourself the help you need and deserve for your sake, and your baby's.

Gimme a break

Gimme a Break!
Your Baby, Your Feelings

Don't let anybody tell you how you should feel about motherhood. Your experience may be different from your mother's, your sister's, your neighbor's, or that of the impossibly well-rested and impeccably dressed mother with the perfect baby who lives down the street. I remember one seasoned mom laughing at me because I complained that my colicky baby wouldn't even let me have a few minutes to finish getting dressed. I'm sure it was funny to her, but I was mourning the loss of the old me while trying to stuff myself into too small pants, get my contact lenses in, and get back to holding a colicky baby for another few hours. I wasn't laughing, and with good reason. It's okay to be grumpy about motherhood—or to think it's the best thing that ever happened to you. It's your motherhood. Feel however you want to feel about it, but if you don't like the way you feel, try to fix it.

Just a minute!

Between the Lines: The Baby Announcement

We welcome baby Jake
even though Daddy wanted to name him Milton,
a great name for a ninety-year-old man, perhaps

Jake's big sister is very excited, too
to extort all sorts of Grandma swag

Mommy is doing well
considering she's only had a total of three hours
of sleep since last Thursday

and Daddy is thrilled
to go to work every day, thereby evading diapers
and spit-up for eight hours

Even our dog, Sparky, is in love with the baby
because he knows it won't be long until Jake
starts dropping food on the floor

Drop by for a visit
as long as you bring dinner and restock the fridge

Or call anytime
. . . anytime we're not desperately trying to sleep

Look for pictures on our Facebook page
as soon as we get the energy to upload them

See you soon!
Or, maybe, at Jake's first birthday party.
We promise to shower by then.

Chapter Five

Zzzzzz: What? Oh, Yeah
Sleeping or the Lack Thereof

 I was barking into the telephone—again.

"Hello!" I shouted, as though I was trying to thwart off evil spirits rather than greet a friend. She knew enough to promise to call back at a better time—a better time that would take months to reach. When you're not sleeping much for weeks or months at a time, there is no good time for people to call you.

My babies didn't sleep much. Though one was a spectacular napper, his three-hour afternoon

> **Okay, I admit it. . . .**
>
> "I can deal with the diapers, spit-up, messes, laundry, and so on, but I can't deal with going on two hours of sleep a day, that's for sure!"
>
> —*Denise, Mascoutah, Illinois*

snoozes were mostly the result of his less-than-stellar sleeping pattern at night. Sometimes he just needed to catch up on sleep. My other baby, well, he was sixteen months old before we had a showdown that lasted practically all night, until finally, blessedly, he started to sleep through the night pretty much from then on. Along the way, I learned the right way to get your babies to sleep from doing it the wrong way for so long. And now you can learn from the Yoda of Sleepless Nights. Can you feel the Force?

Some parents are fortunate enough to have great sleepers, like the woman who bragged about her baby sleeping through the night "from the beginning," while I tried to find the energy to lift my head up enough to make a face at her. Her baby was even napping through the picnic we were attending, while mine was wide awake. Again. Others, though, need a little help getting their sweet little ones to fall asleep and/or stay asleep. This chapter is for you.

How Much Sleep Do Babies Need?

Age	Daytime Sleep	Nighttime Sleep	Total
Newborn– 2 months	6–7 hours in three– five naps	8–9 hours	14–16 hours
2–4 months	4–5 in three naps	9–10 hours	13–15 hours
4–6 months	3–4 hours in two– three naps	10–11 hours	13–15 hours
6–9 months	2–3 hours in two naps	10–11 hours	12–14 hours
9–12 months	2–3 hours in two naps	10–12 hours	12–15 hours

Ease Your Way into a Routine

While it's true that babies, especially newborns, need a lot of sleep, they often don't do it in large chunks at a time like we do. As a result, your baby snoozes a lot like a cat, waking up every few hours or so to eat and stretch, while the big people are just plain tired. This is normal. And yet, it's often so awfully exhausting.

In the beginning, it's not advisable to try to get your baby to conform to your sleep schedule. She's growing fast, so she needs to eat every few hours, and you need to feed her. So everybody's up often around the clock.

When your baby is a fresh-from-the-hospital newborn, you really can't do much except conform to her schedule. But when she's two weeks old, you can start to teach her the difference between night and day. Here's how:

- **Make daytime more active than nighttime.** During the day, you should make more noise—even if the baby is napping. When you want her to be awake, open the shades, put on music, talk on the phone, run the dishwasher—make the house a lively place.

- **Reserve playtime for daytime.** When your baby wakes up at night, be all business. This isn't the time to play peekaboo or generally make nighttime the right time for fun.

- **Establish a bedtime routine.** Assuming that your babies aren't colicky, thereby making your nights all about getting through the crying, you can start a bedtime routine for your baby. Sing a lullaby, give him a bath, put a fresh diaper on the baby, and so on.

It worked for me!

"We had good luck following the eat, play, sleep routine, so the baby doesn't become accustomed to falling asleep at the bottle/breast. We also did more frequent feedings in the evenings to 'fill up his tank' for the night. Our son began sleeping through the night (nine hours) at eight weeks of age. Heaven!"

—*Sarah, Bloomington, Illinois*

"Be consistent in your routine, no matter what it is. I would feed my babies, then bathe them, and lastly lay them down with quiet-time music going."

It worked for me!

—*Jill, Wichita Falls, Texas*

Let the Baby Fall Asleep All by Himself

I didn't do this. I couldn't do this at first, because my colicky babies cried for hours prior to bedtime until we all passed out on the couch together. And yet, once they outgrew the colic (both at about three-and-a-half months), I started a regular (normal) bedtime routine that worked. It really worked! I could put my babies down in their cribs, awake, and they'd go to sleep with little fuss. (Well, until my younger son discovered he could get out of his bed and walk down the hall. But I cover that little nightmare in *Stop Second-Guessing Yourself—The Toddler Years*.)

Babies as young as two months old can and do fall asleep all by themselves—and not just in short car trips when you don't want them to. It may seem cruel not to rock your baby to sleep. After all, isn't that why you got the rocking chair at your baby shower? But the sooner you get your baby accustomed to falling asleep on her own, the faster you'll get to the coveted full night's sleep you remember so fondly.

Now, some babies fall asleep on the breast or the bottle no matter what you do. You could hit giant cymbals next to their heads, but they're out cold. Some experts might recommend you wake them up and let them fall asleep on their own in the crib, but that seems a bit mean, if you ask me. Besides, I'm not a fan of waking a sleeping baby unless there's a fire or Santa handing out free college money or something.

But if you've got one of those babies whose eyes pop open the moment you put her in the crib, *do not pick her up.* You heard me. She was perfectly fine, well fed, and comfortable when you dared to put her down for the night, right? So what could have happened between the second her eyes closed and the second later when you put her in the crib? Unless you've accidentally dropped a fork in her crib, nothing. Repeat after me: *There's nothing wrong with that baby.* Now, tiptoe out of the room, and let her calm herself down. Chances are, it'll be much easier for her to learn how while she's itty bitty than when she's old enough to get out of her bed, walk down the hall, and chat with you. Trust me. I know.

"Let them fall asleep on their own after the first six or eight weeks. We did this with our second son, and he has no problems whatsoever with sleep."

—Angie, Fredericksburg, Virginia

It worked for me!

"The Marines said it best: Improvise, adapt, overcome."

—Amy, Moore, South Carolina

It worked for me!

READER/CUSTOMER CARE SURVEY

We care about your opinions! Please take a moment to fill out our online Reader Survey at **http://survey.hcibooks.com**. As a **"THANK YOU"** you will receive a **VALUABLE INSTANT COUPON** towards future book purchases as well as a **SPECIAL GIFT** available only online! Or, you may mail this card back to us.

(PLEASE PRINT IN ALL CAPS)

First Name _____ MI. _____ Last Name _____

Address _____ City _____

State _____ Zip _____ Email _____

1. Gender
☐ Female   ☐ Male

2. Age
☐ 8 or younger
☐ 9-12   ☐ 13-16
☐ 17-20   ☐ 21-30
☐ 31+

3. Did you receive this book as a gift?
☐ Yes   ☐ No

4. Annual Household Income
☐ under $25,000
☐ $25,000 - $34,999
☐ $35,000 - $49,999
☐ $50,000 - $74,999
☐ over $75,000

5. What are the ages of the children living in your house?
☐ 0 - 14   ☐ 15+

6. Marital Status
☐ Single
☐ Married
☐ Divorced
☐ Widowed

7. How did you find out about the book?
(please choose one)
☐ Recommendation
☐ Store Display
☐ Online
☐ Catalog/Mailing
☐ Interview/Review

8. Where do you usually buy books?
(please choose one)
☐ Bookstore
☐ Online
☐ Book Club/Mail Order
☐ Price Club (Sam's Club, Costco's, etc.)
☐ Retail Store (Target, Wal-Mart, etc.)

9. What subject do you enjoy reading about the most?
(please choose one)
☐ Parenting/Family
☐ Relationships
☐ Recovery/Addictions
☐ Health/Nutrition
☐ Christianity
☐ Spirituality/Inspiration
☐ Business Self-help
☐ Women's Issues
☐ Sports

10. What attracts you most to a book?
(please choose one)
☐ Title
☐ Cover Design
☐ Author
☐ Content

TAPE IN MIDDLE; DO NOT STAPLE

BUSINESS REPLY MAIL
FIRST-CLASS MAIL PERMIT NO 45 DEERFIELD BEACH, FL

POSTAGE WILL BE PAID BY ADDRESSEE

Health Communications, Inc.
3201 SW 15th Street
Deerfield Beach FL 33442-9875

FOLD HERE

Comments

Get Ready to Rumble

By the time your baby is between three to six months old, chances are he's capable of sleeping through the night. I say *capable* because he might be able to do it, but only if you take the proper steps to make it happen. Also, if the stars are aligned and you win the lottery. No, I'm kidding about that last part, though it might feel that way at times.

First understand what the definition of "through the night" means to sleep experts when your baby is less than six months old. You might think it means turning out the lights at 9:00 PM and then not hearing a peep again until 7:00 AM. Actually, for most babies between three and six months old, sleeping "through the night" means snoozing for a five- or six-hour stretch. But, oh, how that probably sounds like a week on a beach to you right now.

Assuming that your baby is thriving, meaning that she's growing and has no major health issues, she's probably dropped some of her night feedings already. If she hasn't, she might be using her feedings as self-soothing sessions. If you don't mind getting up several times a night, you might let her keep on doing that. But if you'd like to get back to a more consistent sleep schedule, it's time to try some sleep-training techniques. Here are a few of the most popular. (Note: Consult your pediatrician before starting any sleep technique.)

> "I realized my not sleeping was not good for anyone in the family—and I was not sleeping because baby wasn't. So, I let her cry a night or two (under supervision and with a plan) and her body adapted, as did mine."
>
> —Jenny, Poulsbo, Washington

It worked for me!

Let him cry. Also known as "Ferberizing," after Richard Ferber, director of the Center for Pediatric Sleep Disorders at Children's Hospital in Boston, this technique is about letting your baby "cry it out." His theory is that babies need to learn to self-soothe by crying themselves to sleep. Now, you don't shut the door and leave the baby to cry all night. Rather, you visit the baby in ten-minute intervals to tell him everything is okay, and promise that "Mommy's here," and so on, but you *do not pick that baby up*. Dr. Ferber says that the technique works after a few nights, unless your baby is older, in which case it can take longer.

This technique is not for the faint of heart. The moment you shout, "I can't take it anymore!" and rush into the nursery to pick up the baby is the moment you push the "Restart" button. So if you try Ferber's method, make sure you're ready to stick to it. (Of course, if the baby is sick, drop it and start again another time.)

No-cry sleep solution. If the very thought of letting your baby cry it out gives you the willies, perhaps the "no-cry" solution better suits you. Advocates of this sleep technique believe it's cruel to leave a baby alone to cry it out and assert that it actually makes your baby associate sleeping with negative things. Parent educator and mom of four Elizabeth Pantley wrote the book (*The No-Cry Sleep Solution*) on getting your child to sleep using a series of commonsense techniques that focus on determining why your baby either can't fall asleep or fall back asleep on her own. Her "Persistent Gentle Removal System" is designed to help you teach your baby to fall asleep without nursing, bottle-feeding, rocking, or using a pacifier. Some of the commonsense tips include:

Okay, I admit it. . . .

"The worst advice I got was to let the baby cry him- or herself to sleep. We tried this once, and it felt so heartless and awful. Although I wish for some more alone time when it comes to sleeping at night— my kids still come in my room in the middle of the night though they are two and four years old—I think they cry because they need you, and I could never let them cry when they were younger."

—*Amy, Othello, Washington*

• Keep the same bedtime every night.

• Encourage regular daily naps.

• Be consistent with a calming bedtime routine.

Be forewarned that the book is very critical of the "cry-it-out" method, so if the gentle methods don't work for you, it just may add to your feelings of guilt later on if you decide to Ferberize your baby.

Okay, I admit it. . . .

"Do not keep the house silent. Get the baby to adjust to everyday noises (yes, including loud siblings). It may take a week or two for the baby to adjust, but it pays off in the long run. My niece, who has had a white noise machine and complete darkness, can only sleep under these conditions."

—Jennifer, Oconomowoc, Wisconsin

Monitoring baby's sleep cues. Jodi Mindell, Ph.D., associate director of the Sleep Disorders Center at The Children's Hospital of Philadelphia, and Dr. Marc Weissbluth, pediatrician and father of four, each have their own take on this sleep technique, which centers on sensing your baby's sleep cues. Simply put, you watch for your baby to get drowsy, reduce surrounding stimuli (lower the lights, reduce noise), and then put her into the crib awake. Dr. Weissbluth's "extinction" method is essentially a version of "cry it out," where you leave the room, let your baby cry, but you don't return to soothe or console until an hour has passed. He asserts that children have different sleep rhythms that often change over time and advocates strict nap schedules and early bedtimes. He also believes that parents know their babies best. Dr. Mindell, however, follows the Ferber method of soothing your baby every ten minutes.

"Follow the baby's lead and reinforce it. Keep a notebook, so you can see the pattern. When the baby starts the tired cry and rubbing his eyes, stop whatever you are doing and get that baby to sleep. An overtired baby is hard to settle."

It worked for me!

—*Alice, Sugar Land, Texas*

E.A.S.Y.: eat, activity, sleep, and you. Nurse Tracy Hogg, aka "The Baby Whisperer," maintains that babies thrive on routine. She recommends repeating a cycle of feeding your baby, then playing, and then sleeping and, ultimately, taking care of yourself. You soothe a newborn by whispering "Sh-sh-sh" in her ear, which reminds the baby that you're there for her while calming her down. She warns against "accidental parenting," where you reach for a quick fix because you lack the patience for waiting out long-term solutions. These quick fixes, she says, are props, such as pacifiers, swings, co-sleeping, car seats, bottles, and, she says, even the breast. She asserts that using props sets your baby up for relying on them to fall or stay asleep. (Warning: Breast-feeding moms and co-sleepers might not feel the love while reading this book.)

"I followed the method of eat, play, sleep, and that really worked. Sometimes we'd be banging pots and pans to keep her awake. Eventually, she easily fell into the routine."

It worked for me!

—*Stephanie, Las Vegas, Nevada*

Child-centered sleep training. Famed pediatrician Dr. William Sears's *The Baby Sleep Book* centers on following your instincts when it comes to getting your baby to sleep. He suggests that you patiently help your baby to sleep on his own, using co-sleeping, rocking, and nursing your baby to sleep—in other words, the exact opposite of Ferber, Mindell, and Weissbluth. He asserts that sleep must naturally overtake your baby. All you can do is help it along by soothing your baby or letting him soothe himself to sleep. He suggests that you rock a baby to sleep, and never put him down until he's so zonked out, his arms fall limp. In his attachment-parenting style of sleep training, he advocates the family bed and recommends that you carry your baby in a sling during the day, which works best if you don't work outside the home. Under Sears's technique, you never let your baby cry it out. You also don't get much sleep, so be sure you're ready to commit to this program before you dive in.

> **It worked for me!**
>
> "I think five to six weeks is a pretty good time to get baby on a nighttime sleep schedule. If you don't, then you will be at your wit's end!"
>
> —Michele, Atlanta, Georgia

> **It worked for me!**
>
> "Nap times are easier. Just watch for the yawn or eye rub, change the diaper, sing a song, and off to bed."
>
> —Lora, Rochester, New York

Is it Nap Time Yet?

You'll likely start out baby's first year watching him doze off up to seven times a day, and end it contemplating how to push her two naps into one, gloriously long postlunch snooze. At first, it'll seem like your baby does nothing but nap, even at night when you're hoping for something closer to a full-night's sleep. But by the end of the year, no doubt your baby will be awake more often during the day. The trick is to help make that nap time possible without completely turning your own life upside down. Here are some tips for making nap time work:

Be consistent. Just like with bedtime, you need to be consistent with nap time once your baby gets past the early weeks of dozing on and off like a hip replacement patient on morphine. Try to keep it around the same time every day, and in the same place, adjusting slightly as your baby's sleep needs change over time. Now, don't drive yourself nuts if your baby falls asleep in the car once or twice or if you've got to drag her to big brother's pediatrician's appointment at nap time. These things happen. But be as consistent as possible without going crazy.

Don't miss your window. The moment your baby shows signs of nap readiness, including rubbing his eyes, yawning, fussing, and losing interest in people and toys, mobilize. Get your baby ready for his nap right then, or else you might miss your moment. While we adults pretty much stay tired once we get tired, babies can find a second wind simply by spotting a butterfly or after nodding off for a few seconds. The sooner you get him down for a nap, the more likely he'll take one.

Don't make nap conditions too comfortable. If it's too quiet and dark at nap time, it might only serve to confuse your baby. What's day and what's night? Plus, she'll get used to having perfect conditions for sleeping—a dangerous precedent. If it's a little noisy at nap time, she'll learn to sleep through it, boding well for your future in airplane travel, entertaining household guests, and undergoing home renovations, not to mention adding siblings and/or pets.

When all else fails, go for a drive. My mother-in-law would not agree with this one, but I'm saying it anyway: if your baby is overtired but won't go down at home, take him for a drive until he falls asleep. Sleep experts say car seat sleep isn't as restorative as crib sleep, but they also say it's okay once in a while. If you start doing this every day, though, you're training your baby to sleep only in the car, which is a whole other can of worms that I'm certain you won't want to open. But when all else fails, do it (every now and then).

> "Try to keep the napping around the same time every day, even on the weekends."
>
> —*Danielle, Franklin, Ohio*

It worked for me!

> "Don't waste time doing what doesn't work. If the book says to do something, and it doesn't work, then don't do it."
>
> —*Angela, Columbus, Ohio*

It worked for me!

Cut Yourself Some Slack

I have to admit that while I was researching this chapter, a flood of old, bad feelings came back to me. I watched videos of doctors insisting that their methods of getting kids to sleep work. I read through the science behind it and the testimonials from satisfied parents, and I started to think there must have been something wrong with me when I tried—and failed—to get my babies to sleep through the night for too long.

And then I read reviews by parents who said they felt like losers when this technique or that didn't work for them. That's when I realized that we shouldn't have to feel that way at all. Babies, like grown-ups, are different. Some sleep well, and others don't. Some respond to crying it out, and others do better while co-sleeping. There is no one solution, no one answer for every single baby out there, nor for every single parent. The important thing is that you don't keep doing something that's not working. Give it a go for a reasonable period of time, of course. But if it doesn't work, you didn't fail; the technique did. And there's no reason you (or I) should feel bad about that.

Okay, I admit it. . . .

"You can hold babies too much. If the only way they will sleep is in your arms, you've reached that point!"

—*Rachel, Westminster, Maryland*

Okay, I admit it. . . .

"I'm hoping to do better with baby number two."

—*Danielle, Greentown, Indiana*

Gimme a break

Wait Until the Colic Ends

If your baby has colic, inconsolable and unexplained bouts of crying, it can be difficult to get into a regular bedtime routine, because most colicky babies cry at night. My younger son cried from 4:00 until 10:00 PM for months. So I concentrated on getting a nap time routine down pat. It allowed me some control when I otherwise felt so helpless. But you don't have to wait for the colic to end to ease into a bedtime routine. As your baby's nighttime crying lessens over time, take small steps toward instituting a more normal bedtime pattern. Even if it's as simple as soothing your baby in her room instead of on the couch, it's a start toward good bedtime habits that will become easier as time goes by. Soon enough, you'll be able to add a bath time, a book, and even a quiet, peaceful hug. You'll see!

Okay, I admit it. . . .

"It's so much harder for you than for them. They will get used to a sleep schedule if you are consistent. You may spend a few hours leaning on the outside of bedroom doors, crying. They will be okay . . . you will be okay. . . ."

—*Paula, Worth, Illinois*

Just a minute!

The Sleep Deprivation Blues

My baby barely snoozes
When it's time for a nap.
He only dozes off in the car
After we leave babyGap.
I've got the sleep deprivation blues.
The crying, the feeding, the diapers, the mess.
I drive him around till he sleeps, I confess.
I've got the sleep deprivation blues.

My baby thinks his nights are days,
And our days are so long, it's true.
He keeps me up all night
Like we're a family of raccoons.
I've got the sleep deprivation blues.
The crying, the feeding, the diapers, the mess.
Sometimes I unplug the baby monitor, I confess.
I've got the sleep deprivation blues.

My baby falls asleep in my arms.
I can count on it.
But as soon as I put him in the crib,
His eyes pop open, the little . . .
I've got the sleep deprivation blues.
The crying, the feeding, the diapers, the mess.
Sometimes I lie about our bedtime success.
I've got the sleep deprivation blues.
The crying, the feeding, the diapers, the mess.
You can get him to sleep? Wow, I'm impressed.
I've got the sleep deprivation blues.
Oh, yeah.

Chapter Six

Baby-Proofing:
Keeping Your Baby Safe in and Outside the Home

"Watching your children is the most effective child-proof device. You have to be one step ahead of them. Just because they can't climb over that gate at breakfast doesn't mean they won't have mastered it by lunchtime."

It worked for me!

—*Jodi, Pottsville, Pennsylvania*

The moment my baby crawled, backward, under the couch was the moment I looked at baby-proofing my house in an entirely new way—a way that scared the bejesus out of me. Before, I'd protected my baby from things in the house. Now, I'd have to protect him from himself.

When you first bring home your little bundle of inactivity, you might think you're months away from needing to baby-proof your house, but you might not be. Even babies who don't crawl can get into trouble, especially if there are pets and siblings around to aid and abet them. Chances are, you don't need to put everything up on the higher shelves just yet, but eventually, you will. Here's a commonsense guide to baby-proofing your house with tips and tricks from moms just like you.

> "Make sure you vacuum often. Babies find stuff on the floor you can't see. Also look under the couch and tables, stuff rolls under there that you'll never find, but they find it in a second!"
>
> —Denise, Mascoutah, Illinois

It worked for me!

Start with the Ride Home

Before you run around putting plug covers on all the outlets for a newborn who can't see past his nose, let alone find your outlets, think about the first days your baby will have in the house. Start with the ride home from the hospital. Most states require you to place your newborn into a semi-inclined, rear-facing infant car seat before driving him home. Most parents will get new car seats as baby shower gifts, but if you get a hand-me-down, make sure it's not more than five-years-old, as the older models aren't as secure as the newer ones. And make sure it's never been involved in a car accident. Next, install the seat properly—always in the backseat and facing backward. Some 80 percent of car seats are installed incorrectly, so it's a good idea to get a professional to check yours out. You can call 1-866-SEAT-CHECK or visit the National Highway Traffic Safety Administration's website (www.nhtsa.dot.gov) for a car seat fitting location near you. Just plug in your zip code or pick your state, and you'll find a list of locations, mostly police stations, in your area where you can have your car seat checked.

In Canada, each province has its own laws regarding car seats, so check with your local government. Note that car seats purchased in the United States may not be approved in Canada or covered by Canadian insurance. Car seat inspection clinics are run by provinces, local governments, insurance companies, and car dealerships, so check your local area.

In most areas within the United States and Canada, babies are required to ride in rear-facing infant car seats until they reach one year old *and* twenty pounds, which causes a dilemma if your baby is the one with his legs hanging off the car seat. In that case, the American Academy of Pediatrics recommends that you use a convertible car seat, which can be used in both rear- and forward-facing positions with babies who weigh up to forty pounds.

Car seat laws and features change frequently, so make sure you're on top of the latest by checking with your pediatrician and searching online.

"Take the little white plastic protectors off the doorstops, because your baby will get them off and pop them in his or her mouth."

It worked for me!

—Carrie, Louisville, Kentucky

"Make it easy on yourself. Just get rid of the knickknacks."

It worked for me!

—Jenny, Poulsbo, Washington

Think Like a Baby

Imagine you're in a brand-new world where everything is novel and exciting, where the colors are amazing, and all that lies before you is fascinating. Then imagine you want to put it all in your mouth, and you pretty much know what it feels like to be a baby.

One of the most popular tips for baby-proofing is to get down on your hands and knees and crawl around looking for trouble. You'd be amazed at the stuff you'll find while you're down there, from dangerous electrical outlets and cords to potential choking hazards, like that penny you dropped on Tuesday but couldn't find, pen caps, and various small items that somehow missed the garbage can and rolled under the couch.

The more mobile your baby becomes—even when she's just barely rolling over—the more you'll need to make your home safer.

Thinking like a baby is just one way to baby-proof your house. Here are some more ways.

Throughout the House

Set your hot water heater at 120°F or lower. This will help prevent accidental scalding at bath time. You might think, "Well, I'll always be careful!" Take it from a mother whose toddler climbed into the sink and turned on the water while she was in the next room changing the baby: don't assume you can always be on perfect guard 24/7 for their entire lives.

Cover the electrical outlets. Many of them are at crawling-baby height and oh so attractive. Let's see what fits in here! Uh, no, let's not. Let's cover them with plastic outlet covers. We even brought ours on vacation, so we could cover up the outlets in our rental house.

Check your smoke detectors/carbon monoxide detectors. Each U.S. state has its own laws regarding how many smoke and carbon monoxide detectors your house needs and where they should be located, so check with local authorities. Installing them is a great project for Daddy, who will no doubt feel like the Great Protector as he wields his power tools, making the house safer for everyone inside. Make sure, too, that you check the batteries on all your detectors on a regular basis, like when the clocks are changed twice a year.

Install safety gates. Put gates at the top of your stairs and in doorways that lead to places where the baby shouldn't go. I had two in the doorways leading from our kitchen/family room area, where I corralled my kids while they were little. The poor cat had to jump them to get to his food in the dining room, but at least it saved his dinner and my good carpets from the kids.

In the Living Room

Make sure they can't pull things down on top of themselves. This means securing the TV and bookshelves, which they may try to climb.

Ditch the tchotchkes. Some folks will say that your baby needs to learn respect for finer things, but I say why let them learn on your nice things? Put away the tempting knickknacks until your baby is old enough not to beat them up or otherwise ruin them. It's safer for your stuff and for your baby.

Roll up the blind cords. They are a strangling hazard. You can buy plastic holders that allow you to roll stringed cords into them.

Cover up those corners. Some parents swear by the padded table corners and protectors you can buy. Others find them either too unsightly or just plain useless. Take it from someone who suffered fourteen stitches next to her eye, thanks to a coffee table and running in the house, at age six: move the darn thing out of the living room until your baby is much better at walking.

"I moved everything dangerous to a baby from my lower cabinets to my upper cabinets. Now my kids can get into any cabinet, and it entertains them while I clean, make dinner, and so on. It sure beats having all the cabinets locked!"

It worked for me!

—Kelli, Wheaton, Illinois

"Keep a watchful eye, as the bar keeps needing to be raised. One day my daughter just suddenly reached for the dinner table. Whoa! Time to move the fragile items off the center and onto a higher shelf."

It worked for me!

—Sarah, Kindsbach, New Jersey

In the Kitchen

Lock up your cleaning supplies. Better yet, move them to a high cabinet and then lock them up. Even natural cleaners can be dangerous if consumed in large quantities, so move those, too.

Keep the phone number for Poison Control readily available. The American Association of Poison Control Centers will direct your call to your local center automatically when you call 1-800-222-1222. Here's what you'll need to tell them:

- How much your baby weighs

- Any medical conditions she has

- What medications she takes

- A description of what your baby swallowed (If it's from a bottle, read them the ingredients. If it's a plant, be prepared to describe it.)

Keep sharp items/plastic bags out of reach. Bags create a suffocation risk, and knives, of course, are a clear danger. Plus, pots and pans can be heavy, so make sure they're out of reach by turning the handles in when you're cooking. It's hard to cook and answer the phone and watch for little hands reaching where they aren't supposed to, so it's best to be careful and vigilant.

Don't let cords dangle. One good tug of the toaster oven's cord and it's going off the counter. Either roll up the cords out of reach, or put appliances away when they're not in use. And remember to return the plug covers to your outlets when you're done using your appliances.

It worked for me!

"We had to employ a few unconventional methods when it came to keeping our pantry door closed. It was a bit unsightly having a rope wound around the door-knobs of our folding doors, but it also saved our daughter from possible accidents."

—*Kathryn, Lufkin, Texas*

In the Bathroom

Never leave your baby alone in the bathtub. Not even for a second. Remember, children can drown in as little as an inch of water. Let the phone or the doorbell ring, or wrap up the baby in a towel and take her with you, but never, ever leave her alone in the tub.

Latch the medicine cabinet. Same goes for the drawers. Your bathroom is filled with lotions and shampoos that can be dangerous when swallowed. Even toothpaste can create risks, as fluoride, consumed in large amounts, can be poisonous.

Keep your baby out of the toilet. I'm not a fan of toilet latches, as my toddlers found their way right through ours, leaving behind the plastic latch affixed to the seat until we remodeled the bathroom. But they've worked for some folks. Otherwise, just make sure you close the bathroom door, using a doorknob cover on the outside of the door to keep your mobile baby out.

Use nonskid mats in the tub. You never know when your baby will get excited about bath bubbles and decide to jump up and down in the tub. Make sure he doesn't go slip-sliding away by using a nonskid mat at the bottom of the tub. Always pull it up and lay it face down over the edge of the bathtub to dry out to help prevent mildew from forming.

Okay, I admit it. . . .

"The toilet seat locks do not unlock when you are in a hurry!"

—*Lissa, Spring Mills, Pennsylvania*

Okay, I admit it. . . .

"Babies will crawl into small spaces just like mice! Watch 'em!"

—*Lesley, Airway Heights, Washington*

> "Don't put anything in your baby's bed! Nothing!"
>
> —*Merin, Edmond, Oklahoma*

It worked for me!

In the Bedroom

Put the crib in the right place. Place the crib away from windows, electrical and shade cords, curtains, lamps, and so on. I heard of one baby using the changing table, which abutted the crib, to climb up and over and then out of his crib, so space your baby furniture at least a few feet apart. Don't hang anything on the wall over the crib, or your baby might figure out how to pull it down on top of herself. Also, raise mobiles (or remove them altogether) as your baby learns to stand up.

Skip the bumper pads. Bumper pads are increasingly considered dangerous. In fact, several groups, including the American Academy of Pediatrics and the U.S. Consumer Product Safety Commission, recommend that you don't use them at all, citing potential dangers, including strangulation from bedding strings and asphyxiation from the padding. Some experts believe that bumper pads, which were originally used to protect babies from too-wide spaces between crib slats, are no longer necessary anyhow, thanks to advances in crib design.

Make your crib "naked." In addition to bumper pads, never put stuffed animals, pillows—even blankets—in your baby's crib, no matter how much your mother-in-law insists your baby needs a blanket. Experts say that any loose, soft items in a crib are a suffocation hazard, even that cute blanket Grandma crocheted for the baby. Instead, use warm feety pajamas or a sleep sack, which is like a sleeping bag that your baby wears.

Ditch the baby powder. Here's another popular baby product that the American Academy of Pediatrics is cautioning parents about. Talc-based powders have small, easy-to-inhale particles that can cause breathing problems, even serious lung damage, when inhaled. And it's hard to keep the powder out of the air when you use it. Though corn starch is considered a better product because its particles aren't as easily inhaled, you're better off avoiding all inhalable products by sticking with diaper rash ointments or baby lotion instead.

Okay, I admit it. . . .

"Don't assume other parents have read the magazines you have—even your own parents! My son fell down stairs at my parents' house and broke his leg because another parent there thought that he'd be fine on the stairs because he could walk. I was busy helping set the table."

—*Jennifer, Oconomowoc, Wisconsin*

In the Garage

Upgrade your garage door opener. Your garage door should include a feature that forces it to reopen whenever an object (or a kid) touches it or is under the door as it's closing. Don't assume that you'll always carry your child inside. They get older, more mobile, and more likely to dash for the driveway.

Dead bolt the dangerous stuff. Lock up power tools, saws, and other sharp objects when they're not in use. Same goes for pesticides, driveway salt, fertilizer, and the like. Assume your little one can get into anything that's not stored away safely in the amount of time it takes you to say "hello" to the mail carrier or a neighbor.

Keep kids from playing where cars drive. Your little ones shouldn't hang out where drivers can't see them. Keep them away from the entranceway to the garage, and watch them closely in the driveway.

Lock up the garage. Make sure your mobile baby can't get into the garage from the house or a side door. Keep those doors locked at all times, even if it means digging up your keys to get into the house. If your baby has figured out how to turn locks and doorknobs, install a dead bolt at the top (and out of his reach) of the door.

> ## Okay, I admit it. . . .
>
> "Be sure to safety lock all your doors! I caught my kids when they were one and two outside near the woods. To top it all off, my son had just recently started walking, and they took the stairs onto a concrete slab! I just kept thinking about all the 'what ifs'! I found them playing in their sandbox."
>
> —*Crystal, Skowhegan, Maine*

Momma Said

WE ASKED: What's the worst thing about having a baby?

"The anxiety. Knowing that you can't protect them from everything but wanting to try anyway."

—*Beckey, Steubenville, Ohio*

Are There Poisons Lurking in Your House?

I don't mean to flip you out and send you on a mad dash through the house chucking out every bottle you own, but as your baby gets older, you need to be aware of potential poisons inside and outside of your home. Not all of these items are poisonous, but they can create problems if ingested by a baby. Here's a list of things you need to lock up right away:

In the kitchen, laundry area, or linen closet:

- Furniture polish

- Bleach

- Lye

- Bug killers

- Boric acid

- Disinfectants

- Detergents

- Spray starches

- Rug cleaners

- Floor cleaners

- Oven cleaners

In the bath:

- Toxic essential oils, such as camphor, wintergreen oil, and sassafras

Okay, I admit it. . . .

"I worry for them, for what the future holds for them, and I wish I could make it all safe and perfect for them."

—*Kathy, Sykesville, Maryland*

- Bleach

- Prescription and over-the-counter medications

- Iron tablets

- Rubbing alcohol

- Nail polish remover

- Shaving cream

- Certain soaps

- Makeup

- Toilet bowl cleaners

In the garage:

- Gasoline

- Kerosene

- Antifreeze

- Paint and paint thinners

- Turpentine

- Weed killers

Safe in the Sun

While most bottles of sunscreen advise against using them on babies under six months old, the American Academy of Pediatrics says you can use small amounts of sunscreen with at least a 15 SPF on babies' faces and hands even if they're that young. But they prefer that you use long-sleeved shirts and wide-brimmed hats instead. And frankly, until your baby is older, chances are you can keep him in the shade and keep a hat on his head.

Keep in mind that most sunscreens are made up of chemicals that can cause allergic reactions. Sunscreens that contain PABA (para-aminobenzoic acid) or oxybenzone have been shown to be especially irritating to skin, though they've been removed from most sunscreens. My older son broke out in a rash with one sunscreen formulated for adults, so stick with the lotions designed for babies. You might be better off using zinc oxide, which is available in health food stores. But, like with any lotion, spot test it to make sure your baby doesn't have a reaction.

What's in the Toy Box?

The U.S. Consumer Product Safety Commission closely monitors and regulates toys, checking them for issues such as strangulation hazards and lead content. But you can help ensure the safety of your baby's toys in several ways:

- Make sure that toys made from fabric are labeled as flame resistant or flame retardant.
- Stuffed animals and other stuffed toys should be washable.
- If you buy painted toys, ensure that the paint is lead-free. Note that lead paint detectors have been found ineffective in finding lead in toys. You're better off buying unpainted toys.

- Avoid older hand-me-down toys, which might not meet current safety standards.

- All toys should be large enough (at least 1.75 inches or 4.4 centimeters) not to pose a choking hazard. Same goes for any parts that can break off the toy.

- Avoid toys with cords or long strings, which could present strangulation hazards to your baby.

- Avoid thin plastic toys that might break into small pieces. They could leave jagged edges that can harm your baby.

- Avoid marbles, coins, balls, and games with balls that are less than 1.75 inches (4.4 centimeters) in diameter or less because they present choking hazards.

Baby Will Be Toddling Soon Enough

As Baby reaches her first birthday, consider bringing your baby-proofing up a notch to toddler-proofing. Soon it won't be good enough simply to keep the bathroom door closed; you'll have to keep little hands from turning the doorknob, too. You might want to relocate the salt and pepper shakers from the center of the kitchen table, because they may well become within reach for a toddler with a kitchen chair and some determination. I go over toddler-proofing in detail in *Stop Second-Guessing Yourself—The Toddler Years.* Until you get a chance to read it, think like a toddler, and you'll be on your way to the next level beyond baby-proofing.

"You will make mistakes. We all do, but it's okay. Do your best, and if you are unsure, ask. You don't want to harm your baby."

It worked for me!

—*Rachel, Bensalem, Pennsylvania*

"Common sense will kick in when you feel lost and overwhelmed."

It worked for me!

—*Adam, Allendale, New Jersey*

Gimme a break

Keep Up on the Latest in Safety

When it comes to your baby's safety, the rules change frequently. The latest and greatest in baby gear might be the hot new thing one day and the biggest recall the next. Stay on top of it all by subscribing to baby product recall lists online. The U.S. Consumer Product Safety Commission maintains a comprehensive (if overwhelming) list of recalled products on their website: www.cpsc.gov. Other sites offer the latest in recalled items by category and time frame, making it easier to search (and causing less of a feeling that the entire world is out to harm your baby). Google "product recall" or "toy recall" and you'll find plenty of helpful websites.

Just a minute!

Redefinition of Common Terms

Now that you've got a baby in the house, you'll see things entirely differently. Here are a few redefinitions in light of your life with baby:

Fine china: pretty plates you got as wedding gifts that you won't use again until you no longer have to duck flying food at mealtime.

Outlets: electrically charged holes in the wall that make you long for alternative forms of energy *right now.*

The dining room: the safest spot for the cat's bowls, making her the only one who ever eats in there.

Coin collection: The reason you never visit your father-in-law.

Toilet lid: Something to open only in an emergency, like a fire extinguisher case or the secret formula for Coke.

Bookshelf: A place to put things way up high; how to teach your baby to climb.

Chapter Seven

Out and About:
Playgroups, Activities, and Just Plain Getting Out of the House

> "My hospital has a weekly moms' meeting. I loved being able to talk to a nurse and to other moms with babies of similar ages."
>
> —Danielle, Greentown, Indiana

It worked for me!

By the end of the summer, I was bored. I was the only mom in the neighborhood with a five-month-old, and I was getting tired of pushing the stroller around the one-mile loop near our house with no one to talk to. You know, besides the obligatory, "See the birdie, Nicholas? It's a blue birdie." I desperately needed to talk to grown-ups.

So that autumn, I signed Nicholas up for a mom-baby play

program. His name may have been on the enrollment form, but really, the class was for me. There, I met a mom from another town whose baby was a few weeks younger than Nicholas. Soon, we were scheduling "playdates" for our boys, which meant that we put our boys in the middle of a pile of toys while we drank coffee and talked about rashes and milestones and newspaper headlines, since that's all we had time to read. We stayed friends until our boys went off to different preschools, we were no longer desperate to talk to grown-ups, and we were busy with school and various activities in our own towns.

Until your baby becomes mobile and remotely interested in making friends, getting out and about is more about your own socialization than his. Still, there's an art to navigating playgroups, activities, and outings that help stave off your cabin fever while serving your baby some good. In this chapter, I'll cover the ins and outs of getting out of the house with a baby in tow.

> **It worked for me!**
>
> "Kids are forced into too many classes and things too early. Join a mom's group like MOMS Club or MOPS (Mothers of Preschoolers) to make some friends for you and your kid."
>
> —Rachel, Woodinville, Washington

"I liked my new parenting class. You could complain or celebrate openly and honestly with other mothers in the same spot."

It worked for me!

—*Kristen, Loudon, New Hampshire*

Here's what nobody tells you about having a baby: It can make you feel lonely at times. When your days are filled with one-way conversations with your pre-verbal baby, not to mention umpteen diaper changes and pushing the stroller up and down the block, you can feel like you've lost a little bit of who you are. But playgroups and play dates can help fill the new void in your social life while introducing your baby to other people and places.

Should You Enroll Baby in a Class?

Contrary to popular belief, baby classes will not necessarily prepare your baby for Yale. Still, baby classes afford a few benefits for your baby and for you. Here are some of the main reasons you might want to consider signing baby up for classes:

- **It's baby bonding time.** An hour without the phone, older siblings, or the dog to interrupt you might help you bond with your baby. If you work full-time, baby classes can afford you special time with your baby, like a weekly playdate for you both. If you're home full-time, you might not really need to concentrate on your baby so much as you need an excuse to put on matching socks and get out of the house.

- **There are grown-ups there.** Nothing cures new mom lone-liness like a room full of other mothers going through the same thing as you. And it's always nice to make friends with people who are faced with similar issues, life stages, and poopy diapers. Chances are, you'll both make friends at baby class.

- **Babies get a kick out of seeing other babies.** To them, it's like finding another planet full of little people who share their affinity for shoving their feet into their mouths. Fun!

- **It's a change of scenery.** Your baby will get the chance to see, hear, and experience new things. And, yeah, you will, too.

- **It's a milestone measuring stick.** You'll be able to see where your baby falls on the milestones chart by comparing him to other babies. It will help you determine any delays or advances in your baby's development. (Warning: Milestones are not a competition and should not be treated as such or else you'll likely lose friends and alienate people.)

- **You can compare notes.** Baby class is a great place to find out that the rash your baby has is probably just prickly heat, that your stroller was recalled, or that the stomach flu is a-comin'.

- **Are we having fun yet?** Once classes start, pay attention to your baby's reaction. If she's bored or overstimulated, you might want to consider a different class, or no class at all. (Hopefully, you've checked the refund policy.)

> "I liked Music Together. It was low-key and low stress, and both of my kids loved it. There were other nice and mellow moms there, so it was fun for me, too."
>
> *It worked for me!*
>
> —*Emily, San Jose, California*

> "I liked Nurturing Your Newborn. It is just a mother-baby group that meets together once a week and talks about whatever is going on in their lives at that time. I don't know how anyone could get through the newborn period without such a group."
>
> *It worked for me!*
>
> —*Jill, Boca Raton, Florida*

What Makes a Good Class?

You don't really need much to make a good mom-baby class, just a clean facility, a nice teacher, and a healthy atmosphere. If you can observe a class or take a free sample class, do it, because it will help you decide if the class is right for your baby and for you. Here are a few questions to answer before you choose a baby class:

1. **Is it clean?** Don't just watch the class, snoop around. Is there a clean place where you can change a diaper? Is the equipment dusty or wiped down? Are babies shoving things in their mouths, and if so, is someone cleaning that stuff off? And are they using harsh cleaners? Think clean and safe and follow your gut.

2. **Is it too loud?** Certainly, a room full of active babies will involve some squeals and crying now and then. But if you add a stereo blasting Barney's top hits, construction next door, and a playground full of school kids outside, it might be too much stimulation for your baby, not to mention a headache for you.

3. **Is the teacher baby friendly?** My sister-in-law left a Story Time class at the library when the teacher made her feel like her active (read: normal) baby boy was too mobile and loud. The teacher should get along with your baby or the class will give you agita.

4. **Is the class too big for your baby?** Twenty crawling babies in one class can make for too much fussing and pooping. Ask if there's a class-size limit—preferably twelve or fewer—before you sign up.

5. **How much does it cost?** Some of these classes can run upward of $250 for ten weeks. Are you willing to shell out big bucks just to get out of the house? Consider that your local library and town recreation department might offer less expensive—even free—classes before you sign up for baby classes.

6. **Is there a make-up class policy?** Babies get sick, it snows, and things happen. Make sure you get your money's worth with make-up classes.

7. **What's the refund policy?** Some classes will refund only before classes start. Others will give you a one- or two-class grace period, while others offer no such policy. Know before you sign the check, or you may discover that your baby hates her new class (or you can't stand the other mothers) after it's too late.

It worked for me!

"We love Itsy-Bitsy Yoga. I love the bonding time and the relaxation 'mom time' that is built into every class. It is my breath of fresh air and calm after every hectic week!"

—*Shannon, Manchester, New Hampshire*

Are Playgroups Right for Your Baby?

Generally less formal than baby classes, playgroups are a great way to get out with your baby. You can set one up yourself or join a playgroup that's already organized. My local mother's group held a biweekly playgroup that met at the firehouse. The upside was that the kids were contained, and the commitment was minimal. If you couldn't make it, you simply didn't go. It was free, so you didn't lose money, and everyone brought so much food to each gathering that it didn't matter if your donuts

Okay, I admit it. . . .

"I didn't like baby classes. I was always jealous or irritated by the group! Guess I'm a weirdo!"

—*Annie, Honolulu, Hawaii*

didn't make it that day. The downside was that the group wasn't limited to babies, so I had to keep mine out of the way of more mobile toddlers and preschoolers. Also, I felt the strong urge to clean the community toys with baby wipes, especially during flu season. But the playgroup was more for my toddler than my baby, anyhow.

If you're considering joining a playgroup for your baby, think about these issues:

1. **Will you have to host it?** While some playgroups meet at a central location, like a playground or the library, others switch from house to house. Ask yourself if you're up for hosting a group of moms and their babies in your home before you sign up for this sort of playgroup. Some people welcome guests, while others feel like it's just another opportunity not to measure up to the mommies. Know yourself.

2. **Do you like the facility?** If your playgroup is held at a central location, check it out first. Make sure you're comfortable with its safety (e.g., are the outlets uncovered, the doors left open?), its cleanliness, and its location (e.g., are you sharing space with firefighters on the job?).

3. **Does it meet at a baby-friendly time?** If it falls smack in the middle of your baby's nap, don't sign up. You'll just end up with a cranky baby (and a cranky you). Some moms like to hold playgroups after preschool lets out, which is often a

nap-unfriendly time. Fit your playgroup to your baby, not the other way around.

4. **Are there bigger kids there?** If you've got older kids, you might want to find a playgroup that works for them and for your baby. If not, you might prefer to sign up for a babies-only program, so you can minimize the mobile madness that comes with toddlers and older kids.

5. **Do you like the moms?** Playgroups can get very cliquey, so if you don't like the other moms, you might wind up miserable. Your baby doesn't really know one baby from another, so make this group more about your social comfort, and you'll both be happier for it.

"Be prepared even when you aren't planning on going somewhere. That way when something comes up out of the blue, it takes minimal effort to leave."

—*Beth, Morris, Alabama*

It worked for me!

"I keep a box in my car that has diapers, wipes, and spare clothes for everyone in it, so even if I forget some things, we're basically covered."

—*Rachel, Woodinville, Washington*

It worked for me!

Get Out Now!

When her kids were little, my friend Mary Jo used to look forward to taking them to pediatrician appointments, because, she said, "It's an outing." I understood completely. Sometimes you just need to get out of the house, and sometimes you don't want to get out but have to. Either way, you'd better be prepared. The smaller your child (and the more of them you have), the harder it is to get out without a hitch. Here are some tips for making your outings run as smoothly as possible:

Plan ahead, but think backward. I always allotted time to get somewhere by starting with what time I had to be there and then working backward, figuring I'd have to search the parking lot for a dropped sock, pull over to find the pacifier at least twice, and perform an emergency diaper change in the backseat along the way.

Like a Girl Scout, be prepared. Restock the diaper bag whenever you come home, so it's ready for the next time you go out. (More on what to stock in the diaper bag next.) Keep extra supplies (clothes, diapers, pacifiers) in your car and at Grandma's, just in case.

Factor in the fussies. Some days your baby is simply going to be fussy. On those days, make sure you have at the ready every make-baby-happy item you have in your arsenal, such as favorite toys, music, and teethers.

Avoid the plague. Well, not exactly the plague, but the latest bug that's going around. If you know that the stomach flu just went through all four kids next door, don't go there for another day or two. You don't have to treat your baby like the Boy in the Plastic Bubble, but try to avoid contagious illnesses, especially when your baby becomes fond of mouthing as many things as possible.

Know when to fold. Sometimes, your baby just has a no-good, rotten day. If you don't *have* to be somewhere (like the pediatrician's office or Thanksgiving at Grandpa's house), consider heading home and trying your outing another day. Yes, this includes baby classes you've paid for and playgroups where, it appears, everybody else's baby is behaving like angels sent from upon high. If you can't calm the crankies, cut your losses and leave.

"Add fifteen minutes to your start time. You will need it."

It worked for me!

—Kellie, Derby, Connecticut

"Lay out clothes and bags and snacks and drinks ahead of time. And know where your car keys are at all times."

It worked for me!

—Emily, San Jose, California

How to Pack a Diaper Bag

How can you pack a diaper bag without appearing as though you're a Sherpa heading up Mt. Everest? First, remember that you're only going out for, what, a few hours? Unless you live in the wilderness, you'll be able to pick up anything you've forgotten that really, truly can't wait until you get back home. Otherwise, here's a list of on-the-go baby basics for your diaper bag:

- Six to eight diapers for newborns, fewer as baby gets older

- Wipes in a travel-sized container (I kept two in case a blow-out diaper used up the first pack.)

- A wipeable changing pad

- Diaper rash ointment

- Two pairs of extra socks (Where do they go?)

- An extra outfit, two if you've got a spit-up king or queen (I usually kept a jumpsuit available, simply because it took up less room in the bag than separates.)

- Plastic bags for dirty clothes and used diapers (I used supermarket plastic bags because they're free and disposable; a more environmentally friendly option is a washable plastic-lined bag.)

- Bottles, if you're bottle-feeding (I liked the plastic flip-up kind that store powdered formula separately from water until you're ready to use them.)

- Two or three burp cloths, because at least one of them will no doubt get all schmootzy with baby spit-up

- Bibs, if you're dining out or on the go

- Baby spoons and baby food, as needed

- A baby blanket

- Toys, pacifiers, books, anything that soothes your baby

- Seasonally necessary hats, mittens

- Band-Aids, especially after baby starts crawling

- Tissues

- Medicines, as needed

- Sunscreen

- Snacks

- A separate container for your wallet, cell phone, and keys that you can pull out and use as needed

- A camera, so you don't miss all those special baby moments (unless your cell phone takes exceptionally good photos)

It worked for me!

"I packed disposable changing pads. You can use them in a pinch in a car seat or stroller if there is a diaper issue at other people's houses, for the surprise poop that falls out of the diaper only that one time, and of course, to protect your baby at those questionable public changing tables when you have no other choice."

—Kellie, Derby, Connecticut

"I also always have a Tide to Go pen handy! I won't leave home without it."

—*Shannon, Manchester, New Hampshire*

It worked for me!

Taking the Circus on the Road

After Playorena class one afternoon, I was busy wrangling a toddler and a baby back into their shoes and outerwear when I overheard the mother of just one (cooperative) toddler say, "How about we go to BJ's today and see if they have any toys for you!" And off she and her toddler dashed to the new warehouse store in our neighborhood, while I was left to search for my two-year-old's shoes. It would be months before I was able to get the three of us to BJ's, and even then it was like taking the circus on the road.

If you've got older kids or multiple babies, you know that getting out the house is now exponentially more difficult. Unless you've got kids old enough to help, not hinder, your ability to leave your home in an orderly fashion, it might feel like a good idea just to stay home until they are. Ah, but there are activities to get to, not to mention pediatrician's appointments, school, the supermarket, and perhaps, day care. Besides, staying home every day all day is enough to make a long hike in the woods with a baby on your back seem like a swell idea—anything to get out. But how can you when you've got a baby (babies) and other smallish kids?

"I have three children. We lay all of our clothes, socks, underwear, and shoes out the night before. I also pack the diaper bag and the girls' book bags for school then."

It worked for me!

—*Kathy, Blountville, Tennessee*

"I'd have my older daughter find the baby's shoes or 'help' me carry things to the car. If she stayed next to me, I knew that she hadn't undressed or taken her hair tie out."

It worked for me!

—*Kristen, Modesto, California*

Ten Steps for Getting Out of the House in One Piece

I managed to repeatedly leave the house with a baby and a toddler just nineteen months older than his brother, and I know that you have to streamline your pre-outing process, or it'll eat you alive. Here are my best tips for getting out of the house in a reasonable amount of time:

1. Give up on the idea of being spontaneous, at least for now. The more prepared you are, the easier this will go.

2. Create a staging area by the door where all the shoes, coats, hats, mittens, car keys, and the diaper bag go whenever you're home.

3. Change it seasonally so that you don't have to hunt down the mittens on a suddenly brisk October day or dig up the swimmies when the neighbors invite you to their pool one early summer afternoon.

4. Now, keep the staging area stocked and at the ready, so you're not looking for a shoe that's ten feet away or a pacifier dumped behind the couch, when you've got five minutes to get out of the house.

5. Repack the diaper bag every night. Make sure Hubby does the same, lest you end up with a poopy diaper or two and nothing to replace them with at the playground.

6. Keep a stash of supplies and favorite things in your car. This means diapers and wipes, yes, but also socks, hats, and doubles of your kids' loveys (teddy bears, books, pacifiers, etc.).

7. Make sure you replace outgrown clothes and diapers from your car stash with new ones once a month.

8. Add time to however long you think it'll take you to get there, because somebody's going to cry, and the baby's head will need to be propped up, and you're going to have to pull over to find the pretzels.

9. Enlist help, especially in the beginning. Bring along a "wing-mom"—a friend or Grandma to help you— when the baby is little or at least until you get the hang of

flipping open the double stroller with one hand while holding the diaper bag in your mouth.

10. Be prepared to abort the mission. If at all possible, cut your losses and go home when the going gets tough. It'll be easier on all of you.

No Place Like Home

Sometimes, you've just got to stay home with the baby even if you had other plans—and not just because someone has the sniffles. Now and then, you need a day without all the running around, and your baby needs it, too. Recognize when you could both use a day where nobody gets stuffed into a snowsuit and the diaper bag lies still. Send your regrets to the playgroup or ask Grandma to meet you in your kitchen instead of at the mall. Hunker down and recharge, so you're ready and willing to get out and about tomorrow.

> **It worked for me!**
>
> "A half hour prior to when you want to leave, get the preschooler completely ready (dressed, fed, potty-break, whatever). Have husband put that kid in the car. You grab the baby and walk out the door (because you have long had everything the baby needs in the diaper bag)."
>
> —Carrie, Louisville, Kentucky

"Shower in five minutes and eat in the car."

—*Karen, Nottingham, New Hampshire*

It worked for me!

Gimme a break

Put Them in Their Place

You've just spent the afternoon frantically singing and nudging the baby to keep her awake, so she doesn't snooze in the car and ruin her nap. You spilled the contents of the diaper bag all over the driveway, missed the pediatrician's phone call about what dose of tummy meds to administer, and bonked your head on the kitchen cabinet. All this, in addition to your usual diaper-changing, baby-soothing, laundry-doing stuff has made for one crazy day. And then somebody asks you, "What do you do all day?" As though being home with the baby is like a vacation. Don't take it lying down (even though you wouldn't mind putting your feet up). Here's what you say: "I feed, clean, diaper, entertain, tend to, soothe, dress, and keep my baby safe. I keep the coins someone left on the table out of her mouth. I oversee her pediatrician's appointments, stock up on supplies, run the house, teach, cook, and carpool. I do everything you'd pay someone to do if you couldn't take care of your baby—and then some." And then walk away. It works every time.

Just a minute!

It's Maddie's First Birthday!
~~What it Really Means~~

Join us for Maddie's First Birthday party, ~~an extravaganza with fanfare not unlike a presidential inauguration,~~ a fun time for everyone!

We'll have pony rides, a bouncy castle, and a waterslide, ~~among the many costly activities she'll nap through, so pack the swimsuits and many, many anti-bacterial wipes.~~

~~We're having a princess theme, but your kid won't get to wear the birthday girl's tiara and we're going to have cake~~ in Maddie's ears, between the slats of my new chairs, and all over the dog's fur.

Please RSVP ASAP ~~or I'll talk about you at Mommy & Me.~~ Kisses from Maddie. ~~And the next day, strep throat!~~

Come for the games ~~that somebody's kid will refuse to play, choosing instead to teethe on the TV remote.~~

Come for the music ~~that will make you wish Elmo had chosen anything but vocals.~~

Come for the food ~~except perhaps the pink icing you'll find in your hair in the morning.~~

Come for the fun!

Chapter Eight

No, Baby!
Setting Limits, Boundaries, and Rules

Momma Said

WE ASKED: When your baby has meltdowns in public, how do you handle it?

"I stay calm and ignore the disapproving stares. Even if they don't want to admit it, most moms have been there."

—*Beckey, Steubenville, Ohio*

I was in the waiting room at my ob-gyn's office when I heard a parent admonish his baby: "Pas dans la bouche!" he said, or "Not in the mouth." Instantly, I was relieved, not only because I realized I'd actually learned something in my high school French class, but also because it was proof that disciplining babies is a worldwide experience. Whether you're a New Yorker, a Parisian, or a Hollywood star, no doubt you've had to tell your baby not to put things in his mouth. And you've had to tell him over and over again.

Some folks think that you can't discipline a baby, because babies don't understand right from wrong. But everyone needs limits, and there are ways to start teaching your baby the house rules now so that he'll begin to understand them for later. Here, I'll go over how to introduce boundaries, limits, and rules to your baby, paving your way to a (mostly) well-behaved toddler and beyond.

WE ASKED: When your baby has meltdowns in public, how do you handle it?

"Grin and bear it."

—Jill, Boca Raton, Florida

"Keeping baby in a sling in most public places eliminated virtually all meltdowns."

—Kristen, Modesto, California

It worked for me!

Waaaaaa! My Baby Is Having a Fit!

Babies cry. They eat, they sleep, and they poop, but they also cry—a lot. Mostly, they cry because they're trying to tell you something, like they're hungry, tired, or sitting in poop. But they also cry when you don't understand what they want or when you don't give in to what they want, like the candy in the checkout aisle or a bottle when they just had one.

One of my sons used to cry every time the tap-dancing bear on *Teletubbies* disappeared. The bear danced, finished, left, and WAAAAAA! My son cried. I still don't know why, but I'm happy to report that he no longer has any tap-dancing bear issues.

Sometimes, though, my babies cried because I wouldn't let them have something, like the pencil they suddenly became enamored of or some equally dangerous object that I swooped in and took away. Sometimes they cried to get attention, like when they wanted me to pick up something (that they'd just thrown ... again) or when they just wanted to make sure I was paying attention to them.

But when do you discipline a baby? Do you? The answer lies in the definition of "discipline."

Discipline, Not Punishment

When I hear the word "discipline," I picture an angry mom washing her kid's mouth out with soap on *The Little Rascals*. But that's not necessarily discipline. That's punishment. And while there may be a need for punishing your child when she gets older (and, say, steals your iPod or serves beer to her high school friends), there's no need for punishing your baby. She's too young to connect doing the time to the crime, anyhow.

But you can begin to discipline—or redirect—your baby's behavior. I'm not talking about issuing time-outs; those won't come in handy until she's at least a toddler. I'm talking about setting boundaries and limits, even for babies as young as two months old.

During your baby's first eight weeks, it's important that you feed her on demand and comfort her cries. But when she's two months old, you can start to steer her toward your schedule by not rushing to pick her up after a nap or by pushing out her dinnertime five or ten minutes. Of course, if this sends her into an all-out bawl, you should put off your plans. Still, you can start to guide her toward eating, sleeping, and playing schedules that suit your needs as well as hers. That said, understand that you can't spoil a baby that young, no matter what your grandmother tells you.

(Note: If your baby has colic, you need to put off your discipline plans until she outgrows it, typically at three months, though it can take longer. For my sons it was three-and-a-half months. For my niece, it was four-and-a-half long, long months. Just ask my brother.)

Okay, I admit it. . . .

"I heard this line somewhere, and I try to keep it in mind because it is very true: No one hears your baby cry as loudly as you do!"

—*Sarah, Bloomington, Illinois*

It worked for me!

"If you can get an upset child away from the situation and focusing on something else, you will have a happy child within a few minutes."

—*Heidi, St. Cloud, Florida*

Mastering the Redirect

One of the best things about disciplining babies is that they have short-term memories. One minute your baby is having a tizzy over the remote control you just took from his lips, and the next he's stopped crying because LOOK! It's his favorite teether, shaped like Elmo, and oh so fun! Now, what were we all upset about? I can't remember.

The younger your child is, the easier the "redirect" is to pull off. Babies generally don't develop their sense of object permanence—the understanding that people and things exist even when you can't see them—until somewhere between four months and one year old. That's why peekaboo is such a hit with babies. They come to learn that Mommy's head hasn't really disappeared altogether behind that pillow, and when their suspicions are confirmed, it's a joyous moment for them.

The redirect works well at first because your baby forgets what he was being redirected from in the first place. But as he gets older, he'll learn (after many, many redirects) that he's not supposed to put the remote control in his mouth.

Some parents would prefer to redirect their babies' behaviors by smacking their hands and saying "No!" But that really just serves to suppress the behavior without teaching them. The redirect, on the other hand, makes your baby *think*. In time, he'll come to understand that he's not supposed to chew on the remote, and he'll stop trying to do that altogether, as long as you're consistent in your redirect.

The redirect is among the first steps in setting appropriate boundaries for your baby. Here's how to do it:

1. Remove the object of desire from your baby's hands, or remove your baby from the scene.

2. "Sell" her on a more appropriate object, toy, or activity by using your mommy-baby singsong voice and shaking the object or displaying the new activity.

3. After about ten or fifteen seconds, your baby will likely forget what the fuss was all about and enjoy the new object, toy, or activity.

4. Sit for a minute. You deserve it.

Don't be surprised if you have to do this several times a day—even with the same objects or activities. Now, some folks would say that you need to leave out that remote control, so you can redirect your baby many times until she learns it's off limits. That's great advice if all you have to do in a day is monitor the remote. But you've got loads of other things to do, especially if you have other kids, some pets, and a house to oversee.

Seek and Destroy, er, Avoid

I suggest that you make your life easier by putting the remote and other objects of your baby's desire out of reach. Believe me, there will be plenty of chances to enforce the redirect, especially at Grandma's house, restaurant tables (salt shakers are fun!), doctors' offices (who ripped the *Good Housekeeping* magazine?), and the supermarket (aisles of redirects ahead). You don't need to leave your knickknacks out to practice the redirect. Besides, safety comes first.

Baby-proof at least one room as thoroughly as possible so that you can put your baby in it with little to worry about. When my kids were babies, we spent much of our time in the sunroom and kitchen area, so I made sure they were very safe by installing gates that kept my babies from escaping to other rooms, rolling up window shade cords, and locking the kitchen cabinets. (For more on baby-proofing, check out Chapter 6.)

But I went beyond baby-proofing by making sure those rooms were nearly devoid of things for my babies to get into. I moved my cookbooks up to the top shelf of my baker's rack. I put away all my knickknacks and moved the cat's food bowls to the dining room. I kept the remote control on top of the TV and locked up the CD cabinet. That way, I didn't have to simultaneously watch my babies' every move while I made dinner around the corner.

In other words, give your baby freedom with limits, and you'll avoid many discipline issues while still cultivating your baby's innate sense of curiosity.

> **It worked for me!**
>
> "Get up, shower, dress, eat breakfast, brush your teeth, and get out of the house before noon. Yes, the baby will cry. However, he will be crying for the next 365+ days, so ignore him for a few minutes at a time while you look after yourself and your needs."
>
> —Alice, Sugar Land, Texas

WE ASKED: What is the best piece of advice somebody gave you about bringing up baby?

"My mother told me that the baby comes to live with *us*, we don't go live with the baby."

—*Rachael, Ballston Spa, New York*

Don't Let Your Baby Run Your Life

Certainly, your baby is the center of your attention right now and should be. But that doesn't mean you should let her moods hijack the whole house. The baby who gets her way every time eventually becomes the spoiled kid who won't take no for an answer, and by then, such bad behavior is much harder to undo. (Ever see a twelve-year-old yell at her mother in front of an entire bridal shower to "hurry up and eat"? I have, and it wasn't pretty.)

You might be thinking, "Oh, but she's just a baby." Also, "She's so darn cute!" Your baby probably won't start "testing" you until she's a toddler, throwing food to see how you react or attempting to dash off in the parking lot. But if you set up boundaries and rules now while your baby is still barely mobile, it'll make disciplining the Terrible Twos much easier for you later.

Start by establishing a schedule. When your baby isn't a newborn anymore, begin by creating a bedtime ritual, manipulating nap times to better suit your schedule, and pushing back feeding schedules to fit into more predictable mealtimes. Wait a few minutes to pick her up at the end of nap time, and don't rush to tend to her when you know there's nothing wrong, and she's just seeking attention. I'm not talking about ignoring your baby altogether. I'm just saying that your baby needs to become less and less the center of attention and more and more part of the household as she gets older.

> "Set boundaries and create structure. I almost felt like a victim of a crazy, sleep-deprived situation, and then it completely changed my life with my son when I realized I was now a parent and that I called the shots in terms of creating structure and our new life together."
>
> **It worked for me!**
>
> —*Stacy, Forest Falls, California*

WE ASKED: What is the worst piece of advice somebody gave you about bringing up baby?

"Spare the rod, spoil the child."

—*Rachel, Westminster, Maryland*

Don't Just Say "No"

If you limit your discipline to saying "no" a hundred times a day, your baby might lose his interest in exploring. Besides, hearing Mommy shout, "No!" can scare a baby. I'd save it for those moments when you need to thwart a trip to the ER, like when your baby is about to touch a hot stove (been there) or crawl headfirst into the lake (done that). Always follow up with a hug, so your baby knows it's the action, not the baby, that made you say "no."

But for those moments that don't require the shouted "no," consider the redirect or a modified time-out. Your baby is too young to be placed in a chair while an egg timer counts down how long he has to stay there. Instead, simply don't reward bad behavior with attention. Just turn your baby away from you on your lap, and don't talk to him for up to twenty seconds. Then redirect him toward a better activity.

Grin and Ignore It

Well, maybe you don't have to grin. But there will come a point where your baby will love to get a rise out of you. If she's pulling all the underwear you just folded out of the laundry basket and tossing it on the floor, don't make a big deal out of it, or she'll get even bigger ideas for getting your attention. Instead, just clean up the underwear and move the basket out of her reach. Don't grumble, grit your teeth, or shout "no!" If there's no danger to your baby, simply clean up her attention-seeking efforts and move on.

WE ASKED: What is the worst piece of advice somebody gave you about bringing up baby?

"Feed them when they cry. Why would I do that? Moms need to figure out what the cries mean, not just stuff them with milk."

—*Jennifer, Dallas, Texas*

"When my baby had a meltdown in public, first I tried to console by singing or feeding or changing the baby's diaper. If that did not work, I would sometimes leave the store. If I was almost finished and just needed to check out, I would tough it out (stares and all)."

—Jennifer, Oconomowoc, Wisconsin

It worked for me!

Get Ready for the Temper Tantrum

You might think you've got until your kid hits the Terrible Twos before you're going to have to endure your first temper tantrum. Think again. Even preverbal babies make demands, and they can resort to the temper tantrum when their demands aren't met. You can try to redirect your baby's inexplicable desire to take the vacuum hose to the pediatrician's office, but sometimes a meltdown ensues. Now you're running late for the doctor's office, and you've got a screaming baby in tow.

This is where a change of scenery comes in handy. It's a version of the redirect that can work if you keep your voice calm and soothing. Take your baby out of the house (and away from the vacuum hose), but don't put her in her car seat yet. Instead, find something outside to show her, like a butterfly, a bright yellow car, a stream, or anything else interesting. Say "Shhhhhh" a few times, and then say, "Look at the birdie!" But do it without any frustration or anger in your voice. You're redirecting her mood by making her feel calmer and less frustrated. When she stops sobbing, put her in her car seat with her favorite toy and/or a snack and head to your appointment.

Momma Said

WE ASKED: What is the worst piece of advice somebody gave you about bringing up baby?

"Walk off if he throws a temper tantrum in public and let him cry it out. He had entire crowds laying down bets in the department store over who would win. He did, of course. I shouldn't have had him out at nap time anyway."

—Amy, Moore, South Carolina

Be Realistic

Don't drag your baby to go furniture shopping at nap time and expect her to behave. She's tired and cranky, and soon, you will be, too. Time your outings so that your baby either plays or sleeps through them. Make sure she isn't hungry, hot, cold, sleepy, or just plain fussy before you make that trip to the store or the bank.

Granted, there are times you've got to bring an unhappy baby out in public or to Christmas dinner with forty of your closest family members. At the very least, prepare yourself for the ensuing misery by stocking your diaper bag with enough diapers,

Okay, I admit it. . . .

"Once in the checkout at the grocery store—where all the candy is—I wouldn't let her have any, and when she melted, I let her go to town. I told the checkout clerk that it was the fault of the store for being so manipulative."

—Dawn, Arnold, Maryland

distractions (toys, books, teethers), bottles, and so on. Stake out a quiet place where you can nurse or simply decompress. But don't expect your baby to conform to your grand plans when it's, say, bedtime or his dinnertime, or when she's especially tired or just plain under the weather.

> "Babies like to stare at faces, so I hung up a Halloween costume mask of a superhero face where he could see it. He would coo at it, smile at it, play coy with it!
>
> —Tanya, Chattanooga, Tennessee

It worked for me!

> "Whenever the baby wouldn't stop crying, *Barney*."
>
> —Patricia, Kokomo, Indiana

It worked for me!

Bring Out the Big Guns.

Do you know the thing that makes your baby giggle the most? That go-to activity or thing that you reserve for when you want to make your baby happy? For my nephew, it's when I put a pillow on my head, say "Achooo!", and drop the pillow on the floor. It's an instant mood-lifter, and so I use it at family gatherings to keep him happy (and to hear his wonderful laugh). Sometimes, the road to good behavior is paved with ridiculous acts performed by otherwise normal adults. The trick is to find out that thing that makes

Okay, I admit it. . . .

"Our son is our first child, and he's a fantastic baby. I find it very irritating that people continue to tell me that 'my next one will be a terror.'"

—Jamie, Des Moines, Iowa

your baby happy, and go to it when you need it the most, whether it's acting silly, singing, tickling, or whatever makes your baby laugh.

It worked for me!

"They sense your moods, so if you can remain calm that rubs off."

—Sarah, Kindsbach, New Jersey

Reward Good Behavior

Also known as "catching your kids being good," rewarding your baby for behaving well can go a long way in reinforcing good behavior. Plus, it's easy to do. Every now and then, praise your baby for doing something right, such as playing quietly or eating finger foods nicely (without, for example, throwing them across the kitchen). If you reward your baby with attention when he does something right, he'll want to do more of that good behavior. But if he only gets your attention when you're scolding him, you give him the incentive to behave poorly.

Okay, I admit it. . . .

"I pop them on their butt."

—Beth, St. Marys, Georgia

"Don't hurt the babies of the world. They are our future."

—*Mallorie, Lenexa, Kansas*

It worked for me!

A Word About Spanking

It's true: the majority of parents spank their kids. Right or wrong, they do, and I'm not about to tell you not to, even though I don't do it. I think it's teaching your child that hitting is okay, as long as you're bigger than the other person you're hitting.

Now is the time to decide if you're going to spank or not—before you get angry and can't stop yourself. Think it through. Is spanking an effective behavior modification program for you, or are you just plain mad and need a way to get it out?

If it's all about your anger, consider other ways of disciplining your baby as she becomes a toddler. Experts say that spanking works only in the short term. In the long term, it can be problematic. But redirection, change of scenery, shouting "No!", and rewarding good behavior are all in your discipline arsenal now. Consider turning to those first before you resort to spanking.

In fact, research has shown that though spanking might work in the short term, it may actually do harm in the long run. A study published in the journal *Child Development* found that kids who were spanked at age one were more likely to act aggressively at age two.

A BabyCenter survey found that today's mothers are nearly forty percent less likely to spank their kids than their mothers were. Of those who "pop" their kids, most start spanking when their kids are between twelve and twenty-three months-old.

"A lady at church told me right before I had my first baby that I should never, ever back down from disciplining my child, and I never have. Thanks, Sheila!"

—*Clara, Henderson, Nevada*

It worked for me!

Gimme a break

Set Your Discipline Tone Now

Think of baby's first year as setting the tone for her childhood. If you're permissive now, she'll learn how to play you. And while it might be cute now to see your baby bat her eyelashes and get her way, it won't be so attractive later when she's browbeating you into buying whatever electronic gadget she wants now (that you can't afford or simply don't want her to have just yet). Setting boundaries and making rules when your baby is barely mobile might seem mean, but it's actually good for her. The entire world won't cater to your child, so don't set her expectations for it when she's a baby.

"Calmly remove him from the situation. Sometimes they just need time to get through the emotions."

—*Alicia, Atlanta, Georgia*

It worked for me!

Just a minute!

The Rules, According to Baby

1. No sleep for the big people.
2. If it's bigger than a coin, throw it. If it's a coin, stick it in your diaper.
3. When naked, move.
4. When moving, stop to get naked if you aren't already.
5. Hog the breasts from Daddy.
6. When in doubt, poop.
7. Fuss till they give up and put on *Barney*.
8. Be cuter than the pets.
9. Shout your requests into the baby monitor.
10. Relocate everything.
11. No shirt, no shoes, no problem.
12. Earrings are like straps on a bus—they're for hanging onto.
13. So are beards, long hair, and boobs.
14. When they want to take your photo, hold out for the free bubbles.
15. Nothing tastes better than a freshly washed foot, except maybe a dirty one.

Chapter Nine

Just a Few More Minutes
Balancing Baby with "Me Time"

> "Go into the bathroom and lock the door. I've been known to do that when I want to have chocolate without sharing."
>
> —*Danielle, Greentown, Indiana*

It worked for me!

The first time I left my baby with my mother-in-law for a weekend, I cried the whole way home. He was eight months old, and we hadn't been apart since I left him in the NICU, when my insurance company kicked me out of the hospital two days after giving birth. My husband and I were going to tour the mansions of Newport, Rhode Island, for the weekend. But on our first trip as parents, we pretty much ate and slept the entire weekend. After all, we were tired.

While we were gone, I missed my baby, and I probably called my mother-in-law too often. I wanted to hear about his every move. What did he eat? Did he play with his favorite toy moon? Is he sleeping at night? Is he smiling? Does he miss me? She humored me by giving me the full rundown each and every time I checked in.

In time, though, I learned how to let go a little and give myself a break—a real break. I learned how to turn off my internal Mommy Monitor (or at least to put it on "Snooze") and to give myself some time off from motherhood. And it did me—and my baby—some good.

If this is your first baby, you're probably thinking that I am a bad mommy. What kind of a mother leaves her baby and goes away? Or maybe you're secretly jealous that I could even pull off a weekend sans baby in the first place. If it's your second or third baby, you might be thinking, *Where can I sign up?*

This chapter is all about balancing your baby's needs with your desire for a nap and, perhaps, eating with both hands free. You can do it. It just takes some planning and protecting your "me time."

"Look sweetly up at Hubby, gently hand him the baby, yell 'Tag!', and run out the door!"

—*Bethany, Spring, Texas*

It worked for me!

It's All About the Baby

You will change, on average, about 2,700 diapers in your baby's first year. You will lose up to—brace yourself—750 hours of sleep, or about a month. You will have less sex, more worries, and a whole lotta guilt. You will be all about the baby, just the way nature intended it. Or did it?

Long before airplanes, the Internet, and branch offices, families lived together so that several generations could help new parents raise their babies. I remember watching an *Oprah* show about how moms were not intended to go it alone when it comes to raising children. The expert on the show claimed that mothers were not meant to get up with their babies all night alone, take care of them all day alone, and feel solely responsible for every little thing that goes awry alone. Well, I added that last part, but really, we mothers, especially new ones, put an awful lot on our own shoulders. Or maybe society does it—or both.

Okay, I admit it. . . .

" 'Me time' as you knew it is gone. I can't even go upstairs to the bathroom without a toddler hanging over the gate at the bottom of the stairs crying like he has been abandoned."

—*Beckey, Steubenville, Ohio*

Anyhow, it all means we can focus entirely too much on our babies and entirely too little on us. That's how come a good friend of mine wound up with walking pneumonia when her four kids were little, why moms put themselves dead last, and why I was cheering at the *Oprah* show, "Amen!"

Now, I'm not saying that you should put your baby down and go outside for a joyride. (Can you have a joyride in a minivan?) Nor do I believe that your baby is better off if you spend your day watching *Flipping Out* reruns and mixing pomegranate martinis. But I do think that there's room for more of you and less of all that baby stuff in your schedule, but only if you make it happen. I also think that a little "me time" for mom is good for you and for your baby. Remember, OSHA has rules about working hours and mandatory breaks for workers so that no one gets hurt. And you need a break, too.

> **It worked for me!**
>
> "Plan ahead. I call my friends a week in advance and let them know that I have a sitter for Tuesday night, and I'm free for whatever. Sometimes it's dinner; sometimes it's just hanging out kid-free at one of their houses. I look forward to it for a few days, and it gets me through some of the rougher parenting moments."
>
> —Kristen, Modesto, California

> **It worked for me!**
>
> "When they nap, grab that time for yourself. Do not do housework during that time."
>
> —Emily, San Jose, California

What Constitutes "Me Time"?

If you're reading this while you're still expecting your baby, be forewarned: this section might scare the bejesus out of you. Until now, "me time" may have meant strolling around the bookstore, venti latte in hand, picking out your next opus to tackle. Or it meant dinner *and* a movie in the same night (back before that would cost you an additional forty bucks in babysitting or the likelihood that you'd fall asleep midmovie). "Me time" means something entirely different now.

The younger your baby and the less help you have, the shorter your "me time" will be. This means that if you get a chance to shave both of your legs on the same day or manage to catch the video of *Saturday Night Live*'s "Weekend Update" on YouTube that everyone's been talking about for three weeks now, you've got your "me time." And on most days, it'll feel like a minivacation.

But as your newborn turns into a baby, and your baby into a toddler, there's often more room for "me time." Barring, say, octuplets or major developmental or medical concerns in your baby, you can find ways to get that time off by turning to other people to watch the baby for you. What you do with that time, however, may be scaled down from what you're used to.

I remember leaving my baby and toddler with a sitter and going out to dinner with my husband. We were so exhausted, we barely spoke, and yet, we were thrilled to be out and not consoling a colicky baby. After dinner, we bought giant cups of coffee and sat on a bench outside the coffee shop, watching cars park. Yep, that was our big night out, and frankly, it's about all we could handle at the time.

As our kids got older, we stepped up our definition of "me time" on our dates, and I expected more for myself. I joined a gym, and my husband took up running. I left my kids with my mother-in-law and spent a few hours skiing with my father. And I spent my nights launching a website for moms. You never know what will come out of your "me time" until you take it.

How to Get Your "Me Time" Now

Here's my five-step plan for finding "me time" when you've got a baby at home:

Step 1: Trust Other People

I put this one first, because I know it's the hardest one for most new moms. First, nature gave you hormones that make you fiercely protective of your baby. Then, the media added fear to the mix by telling of horror stories about bad things happening to kids when they're not with their mothers. Soon, guilt seeped in, and then your husband went and did something really dumb, like putting a diaper on backward or not heating up the bottle before feeding the baby. Your conclusion? Only you are qualified to care for your baby.

But that's not true. All it takes is some trust and a gradual lowering of your standards, and you can safely and successfully leave your baby with other people. Really! Whether it's a day care teacher that you've vetted through interviews and background checks, or your mother, who raised you and you turned out just fine, you can leave your baby with trusted family, friends, and child care providers. And yes, Daddy. I'll go over in more detail your baby's relationship with other family members in Chapter 10. But for now, remember these important points:

- Daddy is not an assistant mother. As long as your baby is safe, let him parent his own way.

- Some of the baby care rules have changed in the past few decades. Certain rules, such as putting baby on her back to sleep, must be enforced, no matter who's watching the baby. Others, though, aren't as important.

- Some folks have more parenting experience than you do. Trust them. They might know something.

Step 2: Give Yourself Permission to Think About Yourself

Starting with the first Baby on Board sign, which probably went on a 1985 Volvo, our society has been particularly childcentric. Too childcentric, if you ask me. Granted, the younger your kid, the more attention he requires. But our generation of mothers has taken baby care to an unprecedented level—a level where there's little room for Mom or her needs. As a result, we're burning out, and it's not good for us, let alone for our kids.

If you're among the more than 55 percent of moms who are home full-time with their babies, you might find yourself falling into the same trap that I did. You might think, *Well, this is my job now, and I'd better be the best ever at it.* And so you sign up for baby classes, create "teachable moments" out of folding laundry, and work really, really hard at giving your baby every opportunity possible, because you're fortunate enough to stay home full-time, darn it. But sometimes, your baby just needs to lie on the floor and study her fingers. And sometimes, you need to do the crossword puzzle and attempt to reach the bottom of your coffee mug for once. And guess what? That's okay. Really.

If you're working from home or at a job away from home, you might get caught up in the idea that if you're not working, you'd better be with your baby and vice versa. But that leaves little room for you, not to mention haircuts or showers or sleep. If you're spending your lunch hours at babyGap or putting off your doctor visits, you're not thinking about your well-being. Your husband likely doesn't feel guilty for working, so why should you? Don't take it out on yourself. Rather, think of yourself as the CEO of the house. You need to take care of yourself, so you can take care of everybody else, too.

> "Don't do everything for your kids. Don't make them the sun that you orbit around; find some balance."
>
> —*Annie, Honolulu, Hawaii*

It worked for me!

Step 3: Give Your Baby Some Room

Contrary to popular belief, you don't have to fill your baby's day with Beethoven, flash cards, and vocabulary building. You don't have to micromanage every moment of your baby's life. The sooner you teach your baby a little independence, the more she'll learn how to entertain herself. And if you've ever spent an afternoon with ten-year-olds who don't know how to play, you'll understand why that's so important.

While it might look like your baby isn't doing much when she's lying on her back staring at her monkey mobile, she's actually learning. And she doesn't necessarily need your running commentary on "the pretty monkey, the brown monkey, the smiling monkey . . ." to get it, either. Sometimes, she just needs to stare at the monkey and, perhaps, attempt to suck on her toes. While this might seem to you the road toward a future as the Village Idiot, it's not. It's your baby taking in colors and shapes and, mmmm, toes.

By the time your baby is old enough to lift her head, she can benefit from tummy time in the playpen or crib, or on a blanket on the floor (assuming you don't have a dog or a toddler to run her over). Meanwhile, you can catch up on reading your e-mail or watching the news. If she fusses, turn her back over and let her grab her toys, babble to herself, or watch the cat clean itself. But don't give up on giving her some room. She needs to learn a little independence, and you deserve some time off.

WE ASKED: What's the worst part of having a baby?

"Losing who I was, body, mind, and spirit, and morphing into a stranger. I turned into Supermom and lost all independence."

—*Paula, Worth, Illinois*

Step 4: Make Time for Yourself and Then Guard It Like a Pit Bull

Until my kids started preschool, my mother-in-law watched them one day a week for me. I knew that Thursdays were my days, and I made sure it stayed that way. That meant that when Omi showed up, I left. I didn't return every hour to see how things were going. I didn't even call (well, in time I learned not to call), unless I was running late on my way home. That was their time, and it wasn't my place to get in their way. It was also my "me time," and I made sure I used it wisely.

Omi-time was easy to take, but leaving my baby with Hubby and going out was harder for me. I knew that he needed his time, too, and it's difficult to mow the lawn and watch a baby at the same time. But if I made plans to go to the gym, I tried not to skip the elliptical machine in favor of a pharmacy run or a trip to BJ's to find itty-bitty socks and a jumbo box of diapers. I could get those things on the way home, and the extra fifteen minutes wouldn't kill my husband. Or I could order them online later along with the bazillion other things we needed.

It's so easy to fill your free time with errands, and, yes, I did that sometimes. I got my hair cut, went to the supermarket, picked up the dry cleaning, and all sorts of other errands that seemed much easier to do without a baby (or a baby and a toddler) in tow. But you need your time, too.

If you make plans with your girlfriends, your mom, your husband, or just by yourself, don't be so quick to cancel them for every little thing that seems so much more important. So your baby was a little fussy before you put him down for his nap. He'll probably wake up fine, and if he doesn't, what's the worst that can happen if you're not the one who's there to get him? Unless you're nursing exclusively, there's no reason why someone else can't spend a few minutes "unfussifying" your baby while you get a much-needed break.

Step 5: Ditch the Guilt

Okay, it's really easy to say and so much harder to do. Motherhood is fraught with guilt, often over things for which we have no control anyhow. I remember feeling like a terrible mother because my baby had circular marks on his chest and stomach.

What had I done? I'd put him in pajamas with snaps made of nickel. It turned out he was allergic to nickel. I felt bad that I had exposed my baby to an allergen, but really, how the heck was I supposed to know it was going to do that to him? In fact, the pediatrician said he hadn't seen a nickel allergy in years. And my son's hands have never broken out in a rash while making change, so perhaps he's over it now.

You can't know everything there is to know about parenting, and you shouldn't have to. You won't be there for every little thing your child accomplishes or fails, learns or achieves. When my niece fell off a swing and broke her arm, her mom was just a few feet away. But I'm sure Mom felt guilty anyway. Imagine if she had been at the movies or a spa or watching TV when it happened? Oh, the guilt. And yet, it wasn't her fault, no matter where she was standing.

The sooner you cut yourself some slack, the calmer you'll become. Motherhood will come more easily to you if you lower your expectations a bit and recharge every now and then.

It worked for me!

"My husband and I made a deal that no matter how busy things got, we each get fifteen minutes to enjoy alone to regroup and focus. It works."

—Rachel, Bensalem, Pennsylvania

"If you have a husband, take turns doing things for yourself while the other cares for the baby—even if it's just a bath."

It worked for me!

—*Danielle, Franklin, Ohio*

Share Your Baby, Take Your Time

Until we're all cloning ourselves like Dolly the sheep, remember that it takes two to make a baby. No doubt, however, that the majority of baby care will fall to you, especially if you've decided to stay home full-time. Even if you're working, though, chances are that you pull most of the child care and household management weight. A lucky few are sharing everything equally with Daddy, and if that's you, congratulations! You're either very smart or just plain lucky. But for the rest of us, the baby care tends to fall on Mom's shoulders all too often.

If Daddy is in the picture—and not, for example, in a Hummer in a battle zone halfway across the globe—now is the time to make sure that he gets his time with the baby, so you can get your time with *Access Hollywood* or your favorite book or the bathtub, whatever you consider "me time." It's not enough for you to feel that you deserve the time; he has to buy in to it, too. Here's how to get Daddy to help out more with the baby:

Don't treat Daddy like a buffoon. You know what I'm talking about. He does something dumb like forgetting to snap the baby's onesie back up, or he has no clue what the pediatrician's phone number is, and soon, you're berating him, sometimes in front of family members and friends. It's the old, "I have to do everything around here," rant, and if you act that way, you will continue to have to do everything.

If he makes a major mistake, one that affects the baby's safety, like giving her honey, then by all means let him know what he's done wrong. But if it's a little thing, don't make a big deal out of it. You're probably spending more time with the baby than he does, so you hit your learning curve earlier than he did. Besides, his standards might be lower than yours so that he doesn't really care if his son is wearing his shirt backward. Unless baby is going for his photos at Sears or you're expecting guests, let him wear the shirt backward. The less you nag, the more likely Daddy will help you.

Don't use the word "help." I know, I just wrote it, but I take it back. When you say Hubby's "helping" you, it implies that you're in charge, and he's doing you a favor, like when a passerby holds the door to Macy's open for you or a friend offers you a Tic Tac. But he is not "helping" you, and as I said before, you didn't make this baby by yourself. (And if you adopted, both of your names are on the papers, right?)

Take it from an author, words matter. If you start out by saying that your husband "helps," you're saying that Mommy is in charge and Daddy chips in whenever he's in town or feels like getting off the couch. Once you fall into that trap, it's increasingly more difficult to get yourself out, and soon you're in charge of everything, and Daddy expects high praise just for cleaning out a baby bottle. And frankly, men deserve more than that.

Don't undermine Daddy. That's right, I said *men* deserve more in parenting. Contrary to popular belief, today's fathers don't want to be treated like second-class citizens (or buffoons) when it comes to parenting. They want to feel confident and capable, but that's hard to do when their wives are undermining them by rediapering and undoing whatever it is they just did for the baby.

More than just treating Daddy like a buffoon, this is when mothers actually set their husbands up to fail by not giving detailed enough instructions, withholding information, or expecting perfection. Here are some examples of what I mean:

- Mom doesn't demonstrate how the baby swing works and then swoops in all indignant when Daddy doesn't fasten part of the three-point seat belt.

- Mom asks Dad to give the baby a bath, but doesn't explain that she's changed lotions because of a rash or forgets to tell him the baby outgrew the infant bathtub.

- Mom reswaddles the baby because she could see 1/64 of an inch of his sock peeking out of the bottom of the blanket, (you knucklehead, Daddy).

Tell, don't ask. Once you start asking Daddy for his permission for time off, you set yourself up for a lifetime of power struggles and disappointment. Daddy is not your boss, and you don't need his okay to take a break.

Granted, you can't just declare any old time to go do what you want to do, leaving him with a colicky baby when he's got a conference call or his poker night. Be reasonable. But be assertive when you need time. Say, for instance, "I'm going to get my hair cut on Saturday morning while you watch the baby," instead of, "Do you mind babysitting while I get a hair cut this weekend?"

First of all, you can't "babysit" your own kids. Second, he might well mind, but that's irrelevant unless he's got some big plans that can't include the baby. The baby can go to the Home Depot with Daddy while you get your gray corrected. But if you ask permission to make that happen, you'll feel guilty about it, and he'll act like he's doing you a huge favor by caring for his own kid. Nip that in the bud from the get-go, and you'll avoid power struggles now and down the road when somebody's got to go to Tumble Tots tonight.

It worked for me!

"I would tell my husband, 'Here's the baby. I'm going shopping.' Don't feel like you have to be the sole caregiver all the time. Dad helped make the baby. He can help take care of her! Give yourself at least two hours to yourself a week, even if you have to lock yourself in the bathroom. Something is better than nothing."

—Denise, Mascoutah, Illinois

"Make it known to other grown-ups around you that you need the time, even if they can just watch the baby at your house while you soak in the tub with a good book."

It worked for me!

—*Beth, Morris, Alabama*

Gimme a break

Save Your "Me Time": Shop Online

If you're spending all of your "me time" doing things for the baby, think again. You shouldn't have to spend what little time alone you can get over at Wal-Mart shopping for diaper deals. I've long shopped online as much as possible. I've learned to Google for coupon deals and free shipping and to bundle my shopping trips into one to save money on delivery. I make sure I'm on the e-mailing list for my favorite stores, so I know when the best deals are. And when all else failed, I made sure Hubby brought home the diapers on his way home from work, so I wouldn't have to give up my precious little "me time."

Just a minute!

Ten Signs You're Coming Out of
Your Postpartum Fog

1. You no longer know the TV schedule from 2–6 AM by heart.

2. Your doctor gives you the "green light" for sex, but you ask for a flashing yellow.

3. Your toddler is using your postpartum donut as a hat—and you don't care.

4. Baby lotion commercials just aren't the tearjerkers they were a few weeks ago.

5. You've stopped calling the baby's bouts of colic, "The Devil's Visiting Hours."

6. Your sitz bath is under your husband's car, full of motor oil.

7. You can see your ankles again, and boy do they need a good shave.

8. You're wearing shoes. And pants—with pockets!

9. It's midnight, and you're spamming baby pictures across the Internet—again.

10. The baby *finally* smiles—and you smile back.

Chapter Ten

All in the Family
Your Baby's Siblings, Grandparents, and Other Family Members

> **It worked for me!**
>
> "Before the baby was born, I bought a large plastic storage box and started stashing away fun stuff to do with my daughter. She was allowed to pick something from the Magic Box after we brought the baby home. We would do something together (or with Grandma) while the baby was sleeping or I was nursing."
>
> —Jennifer, Aurora, Colorado

The more they pushed my baby in the tree swing at my in-laws' family picnic, the more my stomach churned. He looked to me like he was about to pass out, but my mother-in-law insisted that he was just a little tired from all the hoopla. I felt his face; he was burning up.

"It's just from the sun and the summer air," she insisted, continuing to push the swing. But my Mommy Monitor told me otherwise. Soon, I pulled Nicholas from the swing and we left the picnic. When we got home, I took his temperature; it was 101 degrees.

It wasn't the first time one of my son's grandmothers had a different opinion about my baby's well-being, and it wouldn't be the last either. While I've always gotten along well with my in-laws and my own parents, adding a baby to the family tree can create situations for potential disagreement. For some, that "disagreement" can develop into a full-out standoff, often with your kid in the middle. For others, it's just a matter of keeping the peace without losing the battle.

Your baby might change the dynamics of your family, not to mention your friendships and your marriage. You may have to deal with Daddy feeling like a third wheel, Grandma knowing best (or not), Aunt Susie's disdain for all things baby, your 100-pound dog's overaffectionate response to your baby, and a whole lot more. Your baby and your family: perfect together? We'll see.

Okay, I admit it. . . .

"I had to let the baby cry sometimes just so my Hubby could hold him, and I could have some time for myself. Then, if the crying became too much, I'd take him back. Eventually, though, our babies learned they could hang with Dad, too."

—*Beth, Morris, Alabama*

"Daddy was deployed for two months, so naturally Baby preferred Mom. Daddy made sure to help with the routine and getting baby ready for bed, and I made sure to stand back unless he needed my help. It took about a week for Baby to be comfortable with Daddy again."

—Keren, Grand Forks, North Dakota

It worked for me!

And Daddy Makes Three

You're all aglow with new motherhood, your baby lying in your arms practically all day. It's like you're breathing together, one big warm bundle of mother-baby love. Family and friends are calling to find out how "Mom and Baby" are doing, but few seem interested in how Daddy is—few, including you, who's exhausted and busy and completely and utterly in love with your new baby. You figure that Daddy's a big boy and can take care of himself. Also, that he should leave you and your new romance with Baby alone and go do something useful like putting away laundry or mowing the lawn or something else that's not in the same room as you. Let's face it: you're dissing Daddy, and Daddy's missing you.

In the earliest of days with your new baby, it's understandable that you feel like your baby's father is the odd man out. But remember that you're still all hopped up on oxytocin, the hormone that helps your uterus contract during childbirth. It's also known as the "hormone of love," and it is present during sex, though you

"Unfortunately, my husband took a backseat—more so with the second child than with the first. It's hard as a mom of a toddler and an infant to make time, but it's essential to take care of and love your husband as well. I don't want to have to get to know the man I live with all over again when the kids finally move out."

—Beth, Morris, Alabama

won't have any of that for the first six weeks after birth. (All too often, it doesn't get much better from there.) Right now, all your love hormones are directed at the baby. If they weren't, I suspect you might notice what that kid did to your body, making you feel less than warm and fuzzy toward Baby.

But even as the oxytocin wears off, and your baby needs you less and less every waking moment, it's easy to fall into the "dis Daddy" trap. Both of you become so centered on the kids and what needs to be done around the house, you have less and less time for each other, until one day, you're swapping kids in a Burger King parking lot and then rushing off to soccer, piano, dance, lacrosse, or whatever kid activity that's keeping you two from speaking in full paragraphs to each other. It happens to the best of us, but with some planning and effort, it doesn't have to cause a rift between you.

Make Room for Daddy

Whether you've got just one baby or an entire brood, it's never too late to work on your relationship with your husband (or significant other). Here are some tips for making room for Daddy:

Give Daddy power. As I wrote in Chapter 9, it's crucial to make Daddy as equal a partner as possible in parenting. Some folks are able to split parenting 50-50, but for many parents, Mom has more time with the kids and, therefore, more duties. But she shouldn't have them all. Give Daddy the power to be a good parent by letting him (or urging him to—you can't force him to) take charge of various activities, such as bathing the baby, going for walks, taking the baby out on Saturday errands, and so on. If he feels that he's an important part of the family unit, he'll be more likely to invest more time and effort into his relationship with the kids and with you.

> **Okay, I admit it. . . .**
>
> "We both work full-time and have never had a sitter outside of our weekly sitter, so we have never had 'us' time unless his parents are in town. Five years and another child into it, we are now realizing that it's probably time to find a sitter so that we can enjoy each other again."
>
> —*Danielle, Franklin, Ohio*

Carve out "us time." For years, my husband and I had a Friday movie night at home. We'd rent movies, put the kids to bed, and watch something that wasn't animated with talking zoo animals or singing chipmunks. Friends of mine even went so far as to have a weekly night out, complete with dinner at a restaurant that doesn't supply crayons to its patrons, and a trusted sitter to watch the kids. You need time to be a couple together, because the kids will someday leave you, but you and Hubby need to try to stay together.

Communicate. This is exceptionally difficult when most of the conversations you have with Daddy center around poop, food, and

Okay, I admit it. . . .

"Both of my boys preferred their dad at first, and it was heartbreaking. I didn't say anything to them about it, but I would cry about it! Eventually they both turned on to me, and now it's pretty equal."

—*Angie, Fredericksburg, Virginia*

sleep (or the lack thereof). When your lives center around the baby, so, too, do your conversations. But there's more to the two of you than diapers and doo-doo. There are your hopes, your dreams, and your plans for Saturday night. There's tonight's big news headline and what the heck the neighbors are doing with that backhoe in their yard. There's more to life than the baby, and you need to talk about it and how you're feeling whenever the baby isn't hijacking your attention. Make the time and the effort now before your family grows even more and your free time shrinks.

E-mail and text each other. When a child-free friend of mine forwarded a funny video to me, I told her I was going to send it to my husband. She asked, "Don't y'all live in the same house?" Yes, we do, but we have separate e-mail accounts and lots of time apart. So sometimes when I want to reach out to my husband, I e-mail him and vice versa. We use e-mail for scheduling purposes so that we don't forget to put Wednesday's Cub Scouts meeting on our calendars because we were busy rushing the kids around. But we also use it to further our friend-

Okay, I admit it. . . .

"At first, the baby preferred me over Daddy, mostly because I was the food source."

—*Jennifer, Aurora, Colorado*

ship by sending funny photos to each other, making jokes, or just saying, "I love you." We've even texted each other bets on what time we'll get home and the weather forecast. The best part about it is that you don't have to talk over the kids.

When Baby Prefers One Parent over the Other

I was the "it girl" of the house when both of my sons were babies and toddlers. When my kids got hurt, hungry, or just plain hankering for a hug, they turned to Mommy. Part of it was the "mommy magic" my husband swore I had: only I was able to get our colicky babies to calm down by putting their bellies to mine and patting their backs repeatedly. Of course, it took hours every day to do, and my husband was often at work at the time, and so it fell to me anyhow. Because I was a full-time at-home mom, my babies spent so much time with me that they often turned to me, even if Daddy was standing right there when they got the boo-boo.

As they got older, however, they joined the Daddy fan club. At the end of the day, they'd shower Daddy with a welcoming befitting someone who'd been lost in the Amazon and presumed dead, even though I was the one who'd just spent fourteen hours entertaining, feeding, teaching, potty training, and otherwise taking care of them. And frankly, it ticked me off.

Now that my boys are big kids, however, I realize that our closeness to each child waxes and wanes just like with any relationship. Every soccer season, I get closer to my younger son, Christopher, when I coach his team, and then his dad gets closer to him during every Cub Scouts project. My kids turn to me for help with their speeches and writing homework, but Dad's number one when it comes to math and fixing the Wii.

But I realize that's all little consolation when your baby pines for Daddy or wants you and only you, even when you just want to sit in the bathroom alone for a few minutes without anyone crying, "Mamamamamamama!" outside the door. What can you do when Baby prefers one parent over another?

Don't take it personally. I know that's darn near impossible when your baby is writhing to escape from your embrace, holding out her arms, and crying for Daddy, so this one's going to take some work. For some reason, Daddy is fulfilling Baby's needs right now, even if you're the one doing most of the work. If Hubby spends more time with the baby than you do, Baby might turn to him more. Perhaps, though, she just likes how he plays or how he smells or who knows what. But it's a phase that will likely turn again in time. Make sure Daddy knows that, too, especially if he's the one who's not in favor right now.

Realize it may just be your gender. Some babies prefer women, and some like men. It's that simple. If Baby prefers you over Daddy, see what happens when Grandma and Grandpa drop by. He may just like the way women cuddle him, and there's not much you can do about making a ladies' man hang out with men. Or maybe he digs you because you're the one who always serves dinner. As long as you're not opposed to bottles, why not pump milk and let Daddy feed your baby a meal or two a day in a bottle? Then you could get a nice break while Daddy gets to bond with Baby.

"She 'punishes' her dad by withholding affection when he returns from a trip. I am sure to give them one-on-one time. I take laundry to another room, so I am inaccessible. Dad gets on the floor and lets her come to him. She eventually realizes that he's there just like Mommy."

It worked for me!

—Jennifer, Oconomowoc, Wisconsin

"My husband has an aversion to little babies. I think he's afraid he'll break them. So as soon as the kids want to be with him, I roll with it. It makes him feel finally competent with them."

It worked for me!

—Erin, Jacksonville, Florida

Let the odd man (mom?) out spend more time with the baby. If your baby prefers the parent who spends the most time with her, let the other parent have more baby time. If, for example, Baby prefers you, disappear while Daddy takes care of bedtime. It's important that you don't make any guest appearances in the nursery, or you'll blow the entire thing. If, for example, Hubby can't find the baby's pj's , he's going to have to wing it without your shouting, "They're in the laundry basket!" thus reminding Baby that the love of her life is in the house.

Play up Daddy. Sometimes a little propaganda goes a long way. If you're the preferred parent, make a big deal out of when Daddy

Okay, I admit it. . . .

"I have a lot more respect for my mother since I've become a mom."

—*Danielle, Greentown, Indiana*

comes home, enters the room, or is about to take over the parenting duties. Think of it like you're rolling out the red carpet for a big star, and then sell it to your baby. Even with a newborn, you can say, "Here's Daddy" in that singsong Mommy voice before you hand him over to the second fiddle. And if you're the current number-two favorite, make sure Daddy does the same for you.

Observe and fix. Every now and then, have the favored parent observe Baby's relationship with the odd parent out. It might be simply that one parent doesn't hold the baby the way she likes it, or maybe one parent spends his time with baby by planting her in the ExerSaucer and watching the game, thereby not engaging the baby in anything that's fun to her. The trick here is to figure out how to make that not-so-subtle suggestion on how to improve parent-baby relations without making the less-favored parent feel like a bad mommy or daddy.

Okay, I admit it. . . .

"Unfortunately, my mother-in-law was used to making the decisions for her daughters' kids. She seemed to resent the fact that I didn't follow her program."

—*Kellie, Derby, Connecticut*

Keeping the "Grand" in Grandparents

My first son made my in-laws grandparents. That's no small thing, as evidenced by how my husband's parents pretty much treated our son like a messiah every time we had a family gathering. My mother-in-law, who adores babies, would say she could "eat him up" whenever baby Nicholas was in her arms. Instead of feeling left out, I looked at it as a chance to two-fist it at the hors d'oeuvres table. I'm not sure that my baby could have been in better hands at that moment. I needed a break, and my mother-in-law needed to inhale her first grandbaby whole.

My kids are fortunate to live near both sets of grandparents. Through the years, my boys have benefited from all four of their grandparents' personalities and interests. Nicholas, for example, shares a love for art with both my dad and my mother-in-law. My mom talks (ahem, yells from the sidelines) sports with Christopher, and my father-in-law has made both kids very cool playthings, including a go-kart and a toy boat. Just like with my husband and me, their fondness for each grandparent comes and goes, depending on varying interests and whoever is taking them to the bookstore today.

The grandparent-grandchild relationship is a complicated web with Mom and Dad stuck in the middle. Face it, you're the gatekeeper of their relationship, and it can live or die by your whims. That's a heady realization to make, especially when you're a new mother. Suddenly, you have power you didn't have before, and sometimes it feels so good to get back at your parents or your in-laws for past injustices by wielding it. The key, though, is not to use your new Mommy powers for evil, no matter how easy or tempting that might be.

Improving Grandparent Relations

If you're lucky enough to have your baby's grandparents in your life, you'll need to learn to do the dance of balancing your changed relationship with them and their new relationship with Baby. Whether the "grands" live around the corner or halfway across the world, here are tips on keeping everyone's relationship running smoothly.

Make time for the grandparents. Whether you plan a once-a-week get-together or an annual plane trip to visit your parents, make sure you make the time for the grands to get to know your baby. You are your baby's social secretary, after all, and so it's up to you to make it happen. If you can't stand your in-laws, then schedule time to leave the baby with them, if they're willing. That way, they can visit their grandbaby while you get a break from parenting and from your "out-laws."

Trust, but verify. Ronald Reagan said it, but he wasn't talking about whether or not Grandma is putting cereal in your baby's bottle when you're not looking. Parenting has changed since you and your husband were raised. I mean, my mother used to pile us all into the back of her station wagon and drive us around town untethered while my brother did magic shows out the back window for the Mack truck driver behind us. Now that you're a mother, you'll no doubt remember similar scenes—possibly involving roller-skating in the street without helmets—and may conclude, perhaps, that your parents are unfit for caring for your baby.

Though the standards of safety have changed since your diaper was fastened by a sharp safety pin that could pop open at any time, the basics of baby care really haven't. Identify for the grandparents the "deal breakers," those things that are absolutely, positively not allowed when it comes to caring for your baby, and explain why. For instance, explain the latest theories behind sudden infant death syndrome, and then tell them that Baby should always sleep on her back. Make your list and stick to it, and then—and this is the hard part—let the little things go.

Don't sweat the small stuff. If your mother-in-law wants to push your baby in the stroller past a particularly loud construction site, ask yourself if you really need to make the fuss (or if your baby will do it for you). If Grandpa thinks he can calm the baby down by putting on a puppet show that you think will send her into an even bigger tizzy, let him find that out for himself. In other words, jump in only if the baby's safety (or nap time) is at risk. Otherwise, let Grandma and Grandpa do their grandparenting however they wish. And if you can get an hour or two to yourself in the meanwhile, all the better.

Put them to work. My mother isn't much of a fan of babies; she'd prefer to play ball with her grandkids or to take them to the movies. Though she loved her grandbabies, she also loved to run errands. So I asked my mom to pick up all sorts of baby gear for me or to shop for the things I couldn't get out to get, such as bridal shower gifts and Christmas decorations. She loved shopping for me, and I loved the free service.

> **Okay, I admit it. . . .**
>
> "I became more the center of attention for having the baby. Everyone loves a baby!"
>
> —*Audra, Elliottsburg, Pennsylvania*

Don't be a butthead. You are not in competition with the grandmothers for Mother of the Year. Don't butt heads over every little thing, like which baby outfit would work best for the family picnic or whether your son prefers toy trains to who-knows-what. Let them win some, and let it go. After all, they might just be right. Besides, you've got the baby full-time; they're just visiting.

> **It worked for me!**
>
> "Most of my family has small children, so we make it all about the kids."
>
> —*Pamela, North Bergen, New Jersey*

Aunts, Uncles, and Cousins, Oh My!

When my first son was born, suddenly his sixteen-month-old cousin became, to me, a walking, dripping, sneezing container of contagion. And I didn't want her near my preemie. Luckily, her parents understood, having been through the very same feelings about their nephews and nieces when their daughter was born. Other people, though, weren't as considerate. You know who you are.

Adding a baby to the family changes the dynamics between you and your siblings, nieces, and nephews. Suddenly, certain family members think you're a pain in the butt because you don't want the family picnic to start at 1:00 PM—smack in the middle of Baby's nap time. Or they don't understand why you don't want to hang out on their boat with them on Saturday, when the idea of being trapped at sea with a crawling baby sounds like hell on water to you.

Or maybe they parent differently than you do. Say, for instance, your sister thinks breast-feeding is barbaric, while you're a fan of nursing—in front of her. Or your brother-in-law thinks that babies should be stuck in a playpen while the grown-ups discuss the economy or fine wines.

But you can all get along, as long as you identify the things that matter most to you and then let everything else go. Here's what might become an issue when it comes to the baby's aunts, uncles, and cousins:

1. **They don't understand baby safety.** Maybe Uncle John has no kids and doesn't, therefore, realize why you're slightly flipped out because he just left a fork and knife on the coffee table. You could designate him the one to take your baby to the ER, but it's better to be safe than sorry that you invited Uncle John over.

Share your safety rules up front. Make a list of the most important safety rules and stick to them, whether you're at your house or someone else's. For example, my sister- and brother-in-law have a rule that the door to the basement at my mother-in-law's house must remain closed at all times, so that my nephew doesn't tumble down the stairs. We have to remind each other, sure, but mostly, the door stays closed. If anyone watching your baby can't follow your safety rules, don't leave your child alone with them.

2. **They dole out unwanted parenting advice.** Everybody likes to give new parents advice, but sometimes it goes too far, like when your husband's sister tells you that you're parenting your baby all wrong. Maybe she believes in the 7:00 PM bedtime no matter what, while you like a few more hours with your baby at night. Or maybe she thinks you should breast-feed longer/shorter/not at all/whatever it is, you can't win. What can you do?

   Shout it out loud or suck it up. I gave the same conflicting advice in my book on toddlers, and here's why: some things aren't worth fighting about. If a family member picks up your fussy baby when you told her not to and explained that's how the baby puts himself to sleep, you need to speak up. In parenting, this is a felony, and you have to call people on it. But smaller offenses, like when someone lets your baby have an extra biter biscuit or buys her (yet another) stuffed animal, are misdemeanors. These, you might want to suck up. They won't hurt the baby, and then you won't hurt your relationship with your family members.

3. **They've never taken care of a baby.** Long before he became a father, my brother instituted a rule when it comes to other people's babies: if they can't hold up their heads, he won't hold them in his arms. But not all siblings are as careful or thoughtful when it comes to their nieces and nephews. Some look at it as a great way to log in some baby care learning time. And that's great, until they make a big mistake on your kid.

   Oversee it when they're learning with your baby. Whether it's a great uncle who never once changed a diaper or a sibling who doesn't yet have kids, make sure you oversee family members who haven't cared for babies much, or at all. Treat them like mother's helpers, even if they're full-grown adults. Tell them exactly what to do and how to do it. When, for instance, they look dumbfounded at the prospect of folding the baby's diaper down to avoid hitting the umbilical cord stump, explain what it is and why it needs to stay dry. If your newlywed brother and sister-in-law want to babysit for you to practice parenting, make sure you spend a few hours with them getting them comfortable with the baby—and getting yourself comfortable with them watching your child.

4. **They stop inviting you places.** Your annual tradition of going to the movies with all of your siblings and their

significant others after Christmas dinner is one of your favorite things to do. But this year, you were left out because you've got a baby. Or maybe no one wants you and your sleepless baby along on the annual family vacation. Or perhaps everyone else has big kids with big kid interests that don't include your baby.

Find a happy medium. Don't wait to get ditched before you speak up. Now is the time to discuss amicably among your family members what adding a baby to the mix will do to your family's plans. See if you can find a way to be included or to find something new to do together. If, for example, you usually vacation slope-side at a ski resort, suggest that, this year anyhow, you all go to the beach in the summer instead. And offer to find the rental. Also, see if your parents will babysit, so you can go to that movie with your siblings. But don't expect everyone else to come up with the plan. You're the one with the baby. You need to take the lead.

It worked for me!

"I do not see my friends as often, especially those spur-of-the-moment trips to the mall. But I make sure to e-mail, write, and call them just as often."

—Merin, Edmond, Oklahoma

Your Friendships—and Your Friends—Will Change

My best friend and I were pregnant at the same time. Lucky me, right? When her baby was born five months after mine, I wanted to share the secret I'd been harboring for months: this motherhood thing is really hard! Only, her baby slept all the time, and mine cried all the time. Clearly, we weren't having the same parenting experience, and it made me feel like a bad mom. I wondered why motherhood was so much harder on me. In time, though, we each had our own parenting issues that proved that no one escapes the tough stuff of parenting, and we learned we can each help out the other.

Okay, I admit it. . . .

"If they don't have kids, you can pretty much kiss them good-bye."

—*Kristen, Loudon, New Hampshire*

Your friends may react to your baby with great joy and happiness or jealousy and aggravation. You might lose them for a while, or you might lose them for good. You'll probably gain new friends, buddies who will become your "momtourage"—moms (and dads) with kids the same ages as yours who will carpool with you, invite your kids to birthday parties, and generally help out when you need it.

Many of the rules that apply to your family apply to your closest of friends. But it's likely harder to keep in touch with friends now that you have a baby. Only you can decide which friendships are worth what little free time you have right now. The true friends will be there when you come up for air after your newborn needs you less and your baby becomes a toddler. But it takes work on your end, too, so make sure you nurture the relationships that mean the most to you.

 WE ASKED: How did having a baby change the other relationships in your life?

"Our non-baby-having friends had to adjust to spending time with the three of us—we are a package deal."

—*Heidi, St. Cloud, Florida*

"I think I became more nurturing toward everyone. I think I became less selfish and realized how selfish I had been before having kids."

—*Emily, San Jose, California*

Gimme a break

You Can't Make Them Understand What It's Like to Have a Baby

I could have killed him. My then child-free cousin came into the vacation house we were renting together after a late night on the town. He brought with him friends, wine, and noise—noise that, luckily, didn't wake up my five-month-old baby or my twenty-one-month-old niece. But it didn't put any of the parents into a good mood. The next morning, we explained why we didn't do late nights anymore and asked him to find somewhere else to go in the wee hours of the morning. He agreed, but the next year, we vacationed without him. All ended well, though I doubt he truly understood until he had babies of his own. If your family or friends don't understand what it's like to have a baby, don't try to educate them. For some folks, it takes until they become parents to "get it."

Just a minute!

A Mom's Blessing

May the road lull your baby to sleep in his car seat.

May the wind lift your Dora the Explorer kite all afternoon.

May the sun shine warm upon your outdoor birthday party with
27 kids, a giant red cake shaped like Elmo, and a petting zoo.

May the supermarket cashier move like lightning,
preferably before your baby finds the marshmallow
"snack packs" in the sale bin.

May you be able to transfer your sleeping baby
from your arms to her crib
without a fuss time and time again.

May your child be the one at day care drop-off
who's not carrying on,
but isn't happy to get rid of you, either.

May you remember your baby's beloved Teddy bear
before you leave on a six-hour car trip to Grandma's.

May there be cookies when you get there.

May it turn out to be just a cold, and not the strep
throat that's going around again.

May there be clean toys at the pediatrician's office.

May you have at least one uninterrupted
conversation with an adult today,
preferably with someone you love.

May you discover the strained carrots on your
kitchen chair *before* you sit down.

May you buy shoes that don't light up, lip gloss
that doesn't taste like bubble gum,
and a shirt that doesn't have Mickey Mouse on it.

May the telephone wait to ring until after nap time.

May it be your mother, offering to babysit on Saturday night.

May you be able to fit into that sexy black dress you bought
before you were pregnant without sucking in your
stomach until you turn blue and pass out.

May there be enough diapers in the diaper bag,
the right sized batteries when you need them, and
room for one more on the slide at the playground.

May there be enough graham crackers for everybody.

May the rain hold off until the end of your stroll down the street.

And until we meet again, may you get a hug every morning
and a little kiss on the cheek each and every night.

Chapter Eleven

Achoo!
When Baby Gets the Sniffles and More

> "Trust your gut instinct. If something is 'off' with your child, you'll know before anyone else."
>
> —*Kristen, Modesto, California*

It worked for me!

I could tell something was not quite right. My baby, just a few weeks old, seemed a little listless and rather warm. I took his temperature: it was 101 degrees. I couldn't figure out how he could have caught a flu bug considering that, since we had checked out of the NICU, we had hardly left the house. Plus, we had no parade of (germy) relatives or friends coming through, and no older siblings to drool and dribble on him.

189

I was worried. My baby advice books said that newborns' "immature" immune systems aren't as good at fighting infections. I read that a fever in a baby that young could lead to a spinal tap, an invasive and frightening procedure I wanted to avoid.

I called the pediatrician and gave him the fever report. He said to pump him full of fluids (mom's milk, in this case) and monitor his temperature (that is, stick the thermometer in my baby's butt every hour while simultaneously avoiding getting hit by an arcing yellow stream).

After a few hours, his fever broke. And so did I. My poor, fragile preemie had scared the heck out of me once again, first by trying to arrive ten weeks early and then by not breathing when he was born (five weeks early). In time, though, I became an expert at identifying my child's fevers, croupy coughs, and cuts deep enough to warrant stitches. You, too, will become the household Florence Nightingale, thanks to real world experience and lots of reading up. How you handle it all is up to you.

> **It worked for me!**
>
> "My second child had a lot of ear infections, and I didn't recognize the symptoms at first. Here's a tip: if he pulls at his ears until he looks like Dopey the Dwarf, you should probably schedule a trip to the doctor's office."
>
> —Amy, Moore, South Carolina

> "For ear infections, keep baby drinking fluids, and during sleep try to keep his head elevated by placing pillows under the sheet so that his ear won't be bothered. It was a nighttime saver."
>
> **It worked for me!**
>
> —*Rachel, Bensalem, Pennsylvania*

The Dirty Dozen of Symptoms and Illnesses

I could write an entire book on common baby illnesses, but I'll leave the compendium of doom to the pediatricians and medical authors out there. In fact, I recommend that you keep at least one medical reference book on hand, just in case. Make sure it's been published or updated within the last year, because medical information about babies can change quickly.

You can also search the Internet, but be careful. You could do a search on "runny nose" and follow link after link, and before you know it, you're convinced your baby has some rare disease caused by inhaling the pollen from a poisonous flower native only to Easter Island, even though your baby has never left New Jersey.

Chances are you'll spend plenty of time at your pediatrician's office this year, but how do you know when to make the appointment? Here are the "dirty dozen of symptoms" to look out for before you dial the doctor. (Please note: I'm not a doctor, nor do I play one on TV. I am a mom, though, and I subscribe to the edict: "When in doubt, call the doc.")

1. **Change in appetite.** If your baby is fussy at her morning feeding, it doesn't necessarily mean you need to take her to the doctor. But if she refuses to feed or loses interest in food for several hours, call the pediatrician.

2. **Fever.** Call the doctor for any fever of 100.4°F or higher for a baby under three months old. For three- to six-month-old babies, the American Academy of Pediatrics recommends contacting a physician for (rectal) temperatures of 101°F or higher. For older babies, they recommend calling at 103°F, though frankly, I'd probably call sooner, especially if the fever accompanies other symptoms.

3. **Mood changes.** If your baby is lethargic, call the doctor right away. If your baby is irritable or has inconsolable crying jags, call. Of course, if you're deep into colic, which has been officially diagnosed by your pediatrician, you're going to have to play "mood changes" by ear. You'll likely sense when your baby's crying is different than the usual nightly wail due to colic. If you're not sure, by all means, call.

Okay, I admit it. . . .

"My first kid was never sick until the week of his first birthday. My second was sick all the time (it seemed) with colds, fevers, and so on. At first I was concerned, but our doctor reminded me that the first didn't have an older one bringing all the germs home."

—*Rachel, Woodinville, Washington*

4. **Diarrhea.** It's softer and runnier than the usual baby poop. If your baby's diaper is filled with watery poo more than once, call the doctor.

5. **Constipation.** Believe me, you will know more about your baby's pooping habits than you ever imagined before motherhood. So if your baby poops less often for a few days, or if he's having a tough time passing dry, hard poops, he may be constipated. This can be confusing, but if your baby is passing liquidy stools, he might actually be constipated. The loose stools might be all that's passing through the otherwise blocked area. Keep in mind, however, that some babies become constipated when you add solid foods. Rice cereal and bananas, for example, have some binding properties that other foods do not. In this case, check with your doctor as to whether you should adjust your baby's diet.

> "For a GI virus, keep a lot of towels on hand for the puke, and call the doctor for medication."
>
> —*Peggy, Coal Township, Pennsylvania*

It worked for me!

6. **Vomiting.** I'm not talking about a little spit-up now and then. Believe me, you'll know when you're dealing with vomit, likely by all the towels you've just placed in the washer. Now, if your baby has been diagnosed with reflux, you'll need to figure out what constitutes the usual regurgitation and what requires a call to the doctor.

7. **Dehydration.** If your baby doesn't wet a diaper in six hours or longer, or if that (creepy) soft spot on her head has sunk in a bit, call your doctor. Same goes when your baby cries without tears.

8. **Snoogies.** That's the not-quite-scientific term for nasal discharge. If it's yellow, green, or gray, or if it's accompanied by more than a little coughing, call the doctor. Also, if your baby has a cold that affects her ability to breathe, make that pediatrician's appointment.

> **It worked for me!**
>
> "Be sure to keep an eye on your baby if she has a cold because the drainage from the cold can cause ear infections very easily. If your baby is fussy after a bottle or when you lay her down for a nap, a visit to the doctor is in order."
>
> —Danielle, Franklin, Ohio

> **It worked for me!**
>
> "My son had recurrent ear infections starting at about four months old and had to have his first set of tubes when he was ten months old. Always, always, go back for an ear check after the round of antibiotics. Our son was not overly fussy when he had ear infections, so we would think he was fine until we went for a routine checkup, only to be told that he had two burning ear infections."
>
> —Shannon, West Des Moines, Iowa

9. **Ear problems.** Your baby could have an ear infection if he's running a fever, cries more than usual, and/or tugs or pulls at his ears. (Babies do play with their ears, so this action alone probably isn't a symptom of an ear infection.) Ear infections can also cause tummy upset, diarrhea, and a foul odor to the ear. They are among the most common of childhood illnesses, though some kids seem to be more susceptible to them than others.

10. **Rash.** I swear we spent more time at Playorena class identifying rashes than anything else. Most of the time, babies get something simple like diaper rash or a heat rash caused by overheating. (Treat the latter by cooling your baby down, bathing her in about two teaspoons of baking soda per gallon of water and airing her dry.) But a rash that covers a large area or one that comes with a fever may be something more serious, so call your pediatrician.

11. **Eye Discharge.** If one or both of your baby's eyes are pink or red, or if they're leaking mucus, call the doctor.

12. **Naval or penis ooze.** I would think this would adequately frighten the bejesus out of you enough to make you call the doctor, but I thought I'd round out the dirty dozen with this important note. If your son was circumcised, ooze on his penis might be a sign of infection. Similarly, a red and tender belly button that's full of puss might also indicate infection during those early umbilical cord stump days.

"Trust your instincts and don't be shy
about calling the doctor. You probably know
your baby better than you realize."

—Jenny, Poulsbo, Washington

"Don't hesitate to call your pediatrician and
speak to a nurse about your concerns or leave
a message for your doctor if need be."

—Dani, Metairie, Louisiana

Natural Cold Remedies for Your Baby

Cold medicines are no longer approved for children under six, so you won't be able to rely on decongestants or antihistamines to make your baby feel better. Some medical experts have said that multisymptom cold relievers really didn't help children much, and they're not designed to shorten colds, anyhow. You can, however, turn to natural remedies to help relieve symptoms and to make your baby more comfortable. Here are a few. (Note: Please check with your pediatrician before administering any remedy to your baby.)

- **Vaporizer/humidifier.** A vaporizer or humidifier can help relieve congestion by keeping his mucus wet while your baby sleeps. A vaporizer shoots hot steam into the air, while a humidifier produces cool air. Some doctors say that the

warm air is better for patients, because humidifiers don't
boil the water, which may allow bacteria and mold to grow.
But vaporizers can cause burns if the hot water is touched.
Nevertheless, keep both out of reach of your baby, and check
with your pediatrician on which is right for your child.

- **Cold air.** Every spring, my older son had a bout of croup, a
barking cough caused by a virus that narrows the larynx.
Our pediatrician recommended trying to relieve my son's
symptoms by placing him in a steam-filled bathroom, but
that didn't work. For him, the best remedy was to lie with me
by the open door, inhaling the cool evening air. If your baby
has croup, try both to see what works. If his breathing gets
seriously impaired, however, rush him to the ER like we did
when my son was a toddler. Doctors put him on a ventilator
with an inhaled steroid to open up his airways, and soon, he
was breathing more easily—and so were we.

- **Suction.** Also known as "nasal aspiration," this is when you
take that scary looking rubber bulb you got at the hospital or
in a baby care kit at your baby shower and use it to suck out
the "snoogies" from your babies nose. Note that it only
works on the wet boogers. Be careful not to shove the aspira-
tor too far up your baby's teeny, tiny nose, and be quick
about it, starting with the most clogged nostril.

- **Saline.** For dry boogers, you're going to have to do some
(careful) digging, or you can loosen them up with saline

drops, which are available at most pharmacies. Get the kind made for babies and little kids. You can also use a vaporizer/humidifier or a warm bath.

- **Cool bath.** This will help lower your baby's body temperature when she has a fever. Note that, unless your baby is less than two months old, your pediatrician likely won't want to see her for a temperature lower than 100 degrees, possibly even 102 degrees. (Ask the office when to call, so you'll know ahead of time.)

Warning! Skip the Honey

Note that it is never okay to give a child under age one honey, even though it can help relieve cough symptoms. Honey can contain botulism spores, which can cause food poisoning in babies. Honey-induced botulism is rare in infants, especially in North America, but it's better to avoid giving your baby honey. Now, before you go ditch your honey altogether, understand that adults have more mature and more acidic intestines that can generally handle botulism spores from honey. Note that the first symptom of botulism is constipation, followed by loss of control of face and neck muscles. If you suspect that your baby ingested honey, contact your pediatrician immediately.

Warning! Don't Give Your Baby Aspirin

It sounds odd, but don't give your baby any baby aspirin—or any aspirin—as it can cause a rare disease called Reye's syndrome if your child is recovering from a virus. You'll notice warnings on aspirin boxes advising you not to give your child aspirin if she's recovering from chicken pox or flu symptoms. But many doctors recommend that you *never* give your baby aspirin, because you can never be sure whether she's got any kind of virus or not. Reye's syndrome causes pressure in various organs, most notably the brain and the liver, and can result in vomiting, listlessness, irritability, disorientation, and worse. It's most commonly found in kids ages four to twelve, and it's often misdiagnosed as encephalitis, meningitis, poisoning, or other diseases.

> "For teething, chill a damp washcloth in the freezer and let baby chew on it. That worked better than any toy."
>
> —Michele, Atlanta, Georgia

It worked for me!

> "A frozen piece of fresh fruit stuffed inside of a [mesh] food sock worked wonders! Not only was it healthy and nutritious, but much more likable than a frozen teething ring or gooey gum ointments."
>
> —Kathy, Sykesville, Maryland

It worked for me!

Soothing Teething Troubles

You're going to spend plenty of time trying to figure out if the fussing and fever your baby has is the result of teething or something more serious. Teething, when your baby's teeth start to push through the gums, can start as early as three months, though you probably won't see a tooth until your baby is between four and seven months old. Usually, babies get their two bottom front teeth first, followed about two months later by the four upper front teeth. By the time your child is three, he'll likely have all twenty of his baby teeth.

For some babies, teething is painless. Others get irritable and have a hard time sleeping. Most babies will drool when they teethe, and they'll look for things to gum, including your fingers if you let them, because it eases their discomfort. There are a few things you can do to help your baby through teething:

- Wipe the drool so she doesn't get a rash.

- Give her a teether or something else to gum, such as a frozen washcloth. Be careful not to give her something small enough to pose a choking hazard.

- With your pediatrician's okay, give her acetaminophen or ibuprofen for the pain.

- DO NOT rub alcohol on her gums, no matter what your grandmother says.

"My son had a lot of gas, and baby gas drops did not really help him that much. I learned how to help him deal with it by using his pacifier and patting him on the back.

It worked for me!

—Cindy, Hillsdale, New Jersey

"Both girls were lactose intolerant, and as soon as we switched them to soy formula the colic was gone."

It worked for me!

—Kristen, Modesto, California

WE ASKED: Did any of your babies have colic?

Yes, one of them: 23%
Yes, more than one of them: 4%
No: 56%
Sorta: 17%

Colic: The Three-Month Battle
Against Inconsolable Crying

Both of my babies had colic, defined as "episodes of uncontrollable crying in otherwise healthy and normal babies." It affects an average of 20 percent of babies, and there is no cure. One of my babies even cried for upward of twelve hours a day, probably because he simultaneously had reflux. (More on reflux next.) I received no shortage of advice on how to treat it, from administering infant gas drops to placing a cross over his crib to thwart demons. For us, neither worked.

The only thing that seemed to soothe my colicky babies was what I called "mommy magic": I put their bellies against mine and patted their backs repeatedly for hours until we both passed out from exhaustion. It sounds daunting and hopeless, I know. But I'm not going to sugarcoat it like so many parenting books do. Your baby will cry just about every day for hours on end for upward of three months, and you will feel all sorts of emotions that few people will understand, unless they, too, have endured colic.

Personally, I think it's more important to concentrate on the parents than the colicky baby in times like these. There will be few things you can do to ease your baby's crying—and she's not going to remember it. You, on the other hand, will need comfort, care, and frequent breaks. Here are my colic care tips:

1. **Get an official diagnosis of colic from the pediatrician.**
   If you can schedule an appointment during your baby's colicky hours, all the better. If nothing else, it'll get you out of the house.

2. **Find what soothes your baby, even if it's just a little bit.**
   For my niece, it was being walked around in the football hold (face-and-belly down on your arm). For other babies, the bicycle pump—where you rotate their legs like they're riding a bike—gets some air out, helping relieve them a bit.

Others swear by the pacifier, soy-based formula, or the sound machine. Try them all and whatever you can find from friends and the Internet (that's not entirely wacky or just plain unsafe), and you just might get lucky enough to find something that soothes colic.

3. **Take breaks.** This one can be hard to do if you've just gotten your baby semi-calm in your arms. For the love of God, don't ruin it! (And yes, I learned how to pee with a baby in my arms.) But you might want to alternate nights with Hubby or leave your baby with a relative who has a strong constitution and abundant patience while you go somewhere where nobody's crying for a change.

4. **Don't let them blame you.** If there's one bit of advice I want parents of colicky babies to walk away with, it's that you didn't cause your baby's colic. It isn't your nervous nature, the glass of wine you drank before you knew you were pregnant, or your choice of paint color that's making your baby cry uncontrollably. And you aren't a bad mom, either. If anyone tries to lay the blame on you, point out that scientists still aren't sure what causes colic. Then go home and make a voodoo doll of that rude person if it makes you feel better.

5. **Expect a wide range of emotions.** You love your baby but hate the colic. Sometimes, though, you might actually hate your baby, even though you know that isn't rational. He's not crying to annoy you, after all. But enduring all that

crying without being able to do anything about it can make even the most patient of parents come undone. Cut yourself some slack and allow yourself these feelings. You can leave your crying baby in the crib for a while, so you can cool down. But if you feel you might harm your baby, seek help immediately.

6. **Know that the end is near.** Three months feels like an eternity away if your baby has colic. But if you take it hour by hour and day by day, you'll start to see that the end of this harrowing time is near. I remember being able to eat dinner on New Year's Eve with both hands for the first time since my son was born in mid-October. Normally, I held a wailing baby through dinner. By mid-January, though, he'd outgrown the colic, and I got my arms—and my sanity— back. You will, too.

It worked for me!

"For colic, I tried the bicycle leg pump and switched to a special formula. It was expensive, but she tolerated it well for three months, and then we were able to switch gradually to normal formula."

—Jennifer, Oconomowoc, Wisconsin

When Is It Reflux and When Is It Just Spit-Up?

My younger son had reflux for about ten months. It's caused when the valve at the top of your baby's stomach is immature, causing food, breast milk, or formula to come back up shortly after feeding. For my son, it was tricky to diagnose because he also had colic that caused him to cry every day for hours. But his pediatrician was able to identify the symptoms of reflux, prescribing medication to relieve it until he outgrew reflux. Here are some of the symptoms to look for:

> **Okay, I admit it. . . .**
>
> "It's amazing to see how long the human body can go without sleep and still be polite to the mailman."
>
> —Amy, Moore, South Carolina

- Excessive and chronic spitting up and/or vomiting (three or more times a day), particularly within an hour of feeding

- Irritability and crying, especially around feeding times (My baby would start to eat, then remember that it made him uncomfortable and start fussing.)

- Chronic nasal congestion

- Prefering to be upright/fussing when she lies down

- Not gaining enough weight for her age

If your baby is exhibiting two or more of these symptoms, see your pediatrician, who will likely prescribe medicine if your baby is diagnosed with reflux. Note that there has been some controversy around some reflux medications, so do your research before you fill any prescriptions.

You can also help ease symptoms in several ways:

- Keep her upright during feedings, a tricky feat when you're nursing. It's best to keep her head above her waist.

- Feed her more slowly to help prevent or at least limit spitting up and vomiting.

- There has been much debate over whether a breastfeeding mother's diet can cause a baby's reflux. Research has found that mothers can pass along potentially allergenic beta-lactoglobulin from cow's milk through their breast milk. No studies, however, have proven a link between other "fuss foods," such as caffeine, beans, cabbage, and onions. But it might be worth eliminating from your diet any food you suspect is upsetting your nursing baby's tummy to see if there's improvement in his symptoms.

- If you're formula-feeding, try soy-based or protein-free formulas, which may help your baby's sensitive stomach digest more easily.

- Burp your baby often.

- After feedings, keep your baby upright for fifteen minutes. (Yes, this might mess up your sleep plan, but you have to weigh his reflux issues against his sleep issues and come up with a new plan.)

WE ASKED: What questions do you recommend new moms ask the pediatrician about their baby's health?

"Your pediatrician is likely to give you the 'party line'—
what the American Academy of Pediatrics says.
A good pediatrician hopefully also has real-life experience
and will share some of that. Ask 'What did you do with your kids?'
or 'What would you do if it were your baby?'"

—*Rebecca, New Berlin, Wisconsin*

"Ask them anything that you need to ask, and don't feel
stupid or ashamed for doing so. If the doctor makes you feel dumb
for asking, then find another doctor that you feel more comfortable
with, so you feel like you can ask a question."

—*Cindy, Hillsdale, New Jersey*

Your Pediatrician— Love Him or Leave Him (Or Her)

Our grandparents often did whatever their doctors told them to do. Back then, doctors were frequently treated like gods who were never to be questioned. But now, we know better. We know that doctors are human; they, too, make mistakes. Also, we know that there usually isn't just one way to treat an illness.

Nowadays, it's perfectly acceptable and reasonable—if not necessary—to be an advocate for your health and for your baby's health. Consider yourself your baby's personal advisor. It's your job to gather information, weigh options, and make choices for your baby's welfare and health.

If your pediatrician's philosophies on child care or treatments don't match with yours, find someone else. If she rubs you the wrong way or leaves a feeling in the pit of your stomach that makes you wonder whether your baby's interests are truly being met, leave her.

Not every doctor-patient (parent) relationship will be all happiness and smiles, though. It's up to you to decide what's important to you. Bedside manner? Education? Experience? Rave reviews from friends? How easy it is to get an appointment? Here are a few of the issues to consider when it comes to selecting a pediatrician:

> "Keep a list pad on the fridge with a pen handy, so you can write down concerns as you think of them, because I almost always go blank when I get into the doctor's office."
>
> *It worked for me!*
>
> —*Shannon, Manchester, New Hampshire*

1. **Is it a practice or a single doctor?** If it's just one doctor, it might be harder to get an appointment. But if you like only two out of six doctors in a practice, you could wind up seeing someone you don't care for.

2. **Does he have experience?** Newly minted pediatricians are often up on the latest studies and treatments, but more-experienced doctors have personally treated many different illnesses and issues.

3. **Does she encourage you to call?** If you feel like you're bothering the doctor, you'll be less likely to call with questions. Some practices have a nurse's line where you can ask your questions. If the nurse finds it necessary, she'll schedule an appointment to see the doctor.

4. **Is he affiliated with a hospital you trust?** If you live in an area with many hospitals like I do, choose a doctor who works with the hospital where you'd most like to end up in an emergency. Our pediatricians worked at a hospital with a level-three NICU, which turned out to be important for our preemie firstborn.

Momma Said

MOMMA SAID'S community has also offered up quite a few great tips for working with a pediatrician. Here are some of them.

On vaccinations:

"Have them explain all about the vaccinations, how it will feel to the baby, what the ingredients and risks are, and so on."

—*Stacy, Forest Falls, California*

"Know about the vaccines your child will be getting ahead of time and decide as parents which ones your baby will get and which ones your baby will not get. You are in charge of this! (I am not anti-vaccine!)"

—*Stephanie, Las Vegas, Nevada*

On milestones:

"Ask the pediatrician what the next set of goals is that your child should be reaching before his next visit"

—Beth, Morris, Alabama

"Understand the normal milestones of development and question if your baby is not following the charts."

—Marilyn, Bensalem, Pennsylvania

On your doctor's philosophy:

"Never allow your doctor to evade any of your questions. Even the most mundane question is important. I harassed my doctor about everything from cradle cap to head measurements."

—Suz, Longwood, Florida

"What is the pediatrician's philosophy about child rearing? It helps if you are in agreement."

—Stacy, Forest Falls, California

"If you trust your doctor, he or she should be your first source of information. Parents and in-laws mean well, but things change quickly. Things changed between each of my three children, never mind over twenty, thirty, forty years. Plus, they know your child as an individual. For children, advice is not one-size-fits-all."

—Kellie, Derby, Connecticut

"Does the pediatrician see the baby before prescribing an antibiotic? This is huge for me as I don't want to give my baby any unnecessary medication."

—Jennifer, Edgewater, Maryland

On Parenting

"Ask the doctor what you should really panic about—and then really only panic about those two to three things."

—Carrie, Louisville, Kentucky

"Make sure you ask for explanations of words/symptoms that you don't understand. It's your job as their voice to speak up for your kids."

—Leslie, Lindsay, Ontario

"My four-year-old was diagnosed with autism recently, and I wished I had asked the pediatrician to evaluate him when he was three and showing sudden signs of delay. Instead, I trusted the pediatrician when he said he would be fine. I should have trusted my own instincts first."

—Dana, Mission Viejo, California

You'll See: You'll Become a Mom-ometer

Whenever my kids don't feel well, they ask me to check their temperature with my "mom-ometer"—my hand on their foreheads. After all these years of motherhood, my mom-ometer is nearly as accurate as a real thermometer for determining who's going to stay home from school.

You might not feel like it now, but you will get good at sorting out the flu bugs from the colds, the coughs from the croup. The key is to read up as much as you can on kid illnesses, ask other moms for advice, and keep the pediatrician on speed dial. Oh, and tune up that mom-ometer of yours. It'll come in handy . . . aha! Handy! Get it?

"When your children are sick, don't force them out everywhere. Take some time with them to relax and recuperate. Sometimes it can be really aggravating to be home with sick kids, so if you need a minute to yourself just to cry, do so."

—Leslie, Lindsay, Ontario

It worked for me!

"There are a lot of answers out there. Read, but follow your instincts. Every child is different."

—Kellie, Derby, Connecticut

It worked for me!

Gimme a break

When Mommy's Sick

One of the silliest things I ever did was ask my mother to come help me watch my baby when I had what amounted to a mild-to-moderate cold. You know, the sniffles. We wound up talking while the baby slept. I didn't really need her help after all, and I shouldn't have bothered her in the first place. After that, I was much more discerning over what mommy illnesses required help, like when I was pregnant with my second baby and I had a terrible sinus infection. I pleaded with my husband to let me take my head, which felt like a melon in an airplane, back to bed, while he watched our toddler for two hours. After that, I could function better, and he could get to work.

Chances are, Mommy can't get a sick day. That's why I used to be thrilled when I'd get sick on a Friday night—Daddy's home! But if you find yourself under the weather, assess how much help you really need and then *ask for it*. But don't abuse it, or you won't be able to get help when you truly need it.

Just a minute!

Wheel of Babies: A Visit to the Pediatricians

- Gums toy that a sneezing, coughing toddler just dumped on the floor
- Falls asleep minutes before his name is called
- Waits until the appointment starts to create the blowout diaper of the year
- Waits until you're packed up and ready to leave to create an encore of the blowout diaper of the year
- Pees on the doctor
- Grabs doctor's hoop earring like it's a strap on a bus
- Starts wailing *before* she gets her shots
- Pees on the nurse

Chapter Twelve

But What About . . . ?
Extra Help for Parents of Multiples, Stay-at-Home Moms, Starting Day Care, and Other Special Situations

"Don't be a hero. Some may think I am a single mom because my husband travels so much for work, but when I am exhausted, I call someone for help. It is better for both you and the baby."

It worked for me!

—*Rachel, Bensalem, Pennsylvania*

I used to be jealous of my husband because he left me at home to go to work where, presumably, he could carry on conversations with adults and remain seated for long periods of time. A stay-at-home mother of a baby and a toddler, I didn't have such luxuries for quite some time. And though I had my own luxury of being able to stay home with my kids, knowing that didn't always make the job easier—at least not when I was holding a colicky, wailing baby for four hours straight while trying to entertain a toddler who wanted to see if various small objects might fit up his nose.

Whether you're home with your baby, heading out to work, parenting more than one baby at a time, waiting for Daddy to return from his latest tour of duty with the military, or whatever your particular situation is, you've got some special parenting considerations that I might not have covered so far. I've compiled my best tips along with advice from MommaSaid's fans to help you through whatever it is you've got going on in your life with Baby.

 WE ASKED: Tell us something about motherhood:

"Raising babies may not pay a salary,
but shaping the future of America is
a proud accomplishment."

—*Suz, Longwood, Florida*

Stay-at-Home Motherhood

There are more than six million full-time stay-at-home mothers in the United States, though you may wonder where they all are if you're the only at-home mom on your block. Whether you've got a posse of at-home moms to rely on or you're on your own, you're in the minority in this country. And you've got some special issues to consider. If you're staying home with Baby, you'll soon learn that at-home motherhood isn't as easy as it had seemed before you gave notice at work. Here are a few survival tips from me, the creator of "*Please* Take My Children to Work Day," an annual holiday for full- and part-time at-home moms.

Five Tips for Staying Home with Your Baby

1. **Don't stay home.** Honestly, stay-at-home mom is an oxymoron. Once your baby is old enough to be out and about, get out of the house now and then. Join a playgroup (which at your baby's age, is really for the moms), or hang out at the park where you just might meet other moms. Push the baby around in a stroller at the mall or down your street, and you'll see that you will meet people—grown-up people—because so many people love to gush over a baby.

2. **Let Baby entertain herself.** Put the educational videos down and put your hands where I can see them. Just because you can stay home doesn't mean you have to make every waking moment of your baby's life enriching and educational. She needs to learn how to entertain herself—even if that means staring at her fingers for ten minutes. Believe it or not, she's learning something. Just as important, you're reading/cleaning/e-mailing/doing yoga/shaving both legs on the same day.

3. **Remember, the baby belongs to Daddy, too.** Staying home with a baby is a 100-hour-a-week job with no vacation days and no sick days, plus you're on call all night. Get Daddy to

do his part as much as possible, reminding him that an exhausted wife can be a lousy wife. Besides, it isn't just your baby, remember?

4. **Create structure.** You don't have to run your days like a drill sergeant at boot camp, but it's good to have some sort of organized flow to your day once your baby gets past the every-two-hours feedings. Perhaps you always go for a walk after breakfast or give Baby a bath before bed. Add some rituals to your days, and they won't all start to blend together.

5. **Make something "mine."** It's very easy to lose yourself when you're at home all day with a baby. But you need something that's just for you, such as a hobby, a gym membership, a weekly night out with the girls, or a pile of books that you actually get to read. Find something that suits your style, and then stick to it. It'll give you the break you truly deserve.

> **It worked for me!**
>
> "Do what makes you feel good. If it is to sleep when the baby sleeps, sleep. If it is take a bubble bath, then take a bubble bath. Every personality is different, and the age-old advice, 'sleep when the baby sleeps,' is great, but may not be what you need."
>
> —*Kris, Clarkfield, Minnesota*

"I work for about one to two hours, then take a break before the kids get up."

—*Bethany, Spring, Texas*

It worked for me!

Working from Home

A friend of mine was able to work from home with her baby lying just feet from her desk for nine months before it became difficult. Her baby slept pretty much all day, and when she was awake, she didn't do a whole lot anyhow. Once her daughter learned to crawl, though, it got harder for my friend to sit at her computer and maintain clever thoughts and coherent ideas, because she had to pop up from her chair to keep her baby from, say, pulling out all the computer wires.

If you've decided to work from home with a baby underfoot, you've got some special considerations. Here are some tips for pulling it off.

Five Tips for Working at Home with Your Baby Around

1. **Baby-proof your workspace.** Whether you're working with a laptop at the kitchen table or you've got an entire room to call your company headquarters, baby-proof it. Even if you've hired help to watch the baby while you work, chances are that the baby will wind up in your workspace

at some point. The more baby-friendly it is, the more work you'll be able to get done. Add a playpen and/or a toy box to keep your baby entertained while you finish up that report that was due, oh, before nap time . . . yesterday.

2. **Forget normal work hours.** If you're trying to work around your baby's schedule, be prepared to stop and start work frequently. Instead of one fluid workday that runs from nine to five, you'll likely have to build in time for feedings, fussing, and playing. Also, build in extra time for your deadlines. For example, you might have an assignment due tomorrow, but your baby might get the flu today.

3. **Get help.** While all those articles about bringing babies to work might make it sound easy, it can be difficult to get work done with a baby around. Hire a sitter or get a relative to watch the baby so you can have chunks of time when you're just working. If you have to work odd hours, do it. I started MommaSaid by working nights, so my husband could take care of the kids while I worked (or stared out the window; it happens).

4. **Take work seriously.** Never refer to your job or business as a "hobby," even if it doesn't make much money. The more respect you have for your work, the more your family will help make sure you have the time to get to your desk, or wherever you work. Plus, you'll be able to add more work hours when your baby gets older, so it's wise to set up the framework for your work-at-home venture now.

5. **Network.** You never know if one of your neighbors could use your services or products, or if they're hiring people to work from home. Make sure you network, even if it's at Mommy & Me, because you could get work out of it. Create a strong web presence, so you can get work from anywhere in the country or world, if applicable. And nobody has to know you're working on their project and nursing at the same time.

Okay, I admit it. . . .

"I wish someone had told me that no matter how much you plan, how much you decide what's going to happen, it will just happen, period."

—*Leslie, Lindsay, Ontario*

It worked for me!

"The best clue is to watch your baby around the person you are interviewing for child care. If he takes to her or responds to her in a positive way, you may just have yourself a babysitter."

—*Bethany, Spring, Texas*

Starting Day Care or Other Child Care Arrangements

More than half of mothers will return to work at some point during their babies' first year. Finding a reputable day care center or in-home childcare that you trust can be a daunting task that requires research, planning, and organization. How can you make sure you're selecting the right day care center for your baby?

Five Tips for Choosing Day Care

1. **Take a tour.** Ask to see the facility during operating hours. Take note of how the adults interact with the children and whether the babies seem content or anxious, engaged or ignored. Check the baby-provider ratio: there should be no more than six kids under a year to every one teacher, though some parenting organizations suggest a one-to-three ratio for babies. The better the ratio, the better it is for your baby.

2. **Ask a lot of well-researched questions.** Find out if the center is licensed, if they have policies on cleaning the facility, what the staff's qualifications are, what the rules are and more. Also, find out about the fees and what their policy is if you're running late from work. Some centers charge extra for late pickups; others don't even allow them. The more questions you ask, the more you'll get to know the people who might soon take care of your baby.

3. **Take a close look at the activities and games.** Make sure that the toys are clean and age appropriate. See if there are set activities that your baby would enjoy. Find out if the center encourages activity so that your baby isn't sitting around all day. Ask whether they go outside, weather permitting, and check out the playground for safety and fun.

4. **Interview other parents.** Don't just talk to parents whose babies are currently enrolled at the center. Find parents

whose kids are older, and talk to people who left the facility and ask them why. You'll get a good sense of what it's really like day-to-day at the day care center if you get the inside scoop from parents in the know. And always check references.

5. **Don't ignore red flags.** Your baby can't tell you what's happening at day care, so you'll need to be vigilant when it comes to identifying the signs of so-so day care. If the facility doesn't have an open-door policy, lacks age-appropriate (and clean) toys, offers no activity outline or schedule, has underqualified, underpaid teachers, or is dirty and unsafe, run, don't walk out of there and find another day care center.

Five Tips for Choosing a Nanny or Babysitter

Whether you're hiring a nanny or babysitter, or leaving your baby with a relative, you need to take into account these considerations:

1. **Ask around.** A great way to find a good nanny or babysitter is to ask other families for references. You may discover that a family is moving or giving up their sitter because their kids no longer need her. Likewise, ask family members if they'd be willing to care for your child.

2. **Check references.** Candidates from outside your family should supply names and phone numbers for references

with their resumes. If you haven't used a nanny service that handles this for you, run a background check on each candidate.

3. **Interview carefully.** The interview is among the best ways to determine the nanny's or babysitter's child rearing philosophies. While you make the rules when it comes to your baby, it's important that anybody who cares for your baby shares the same ideas about learning, discipline, and schedules as you. Ask the candidate how he or she would spend a typical day with your baby.

4. **Outline what you need.** Do you need part- or full-time help? Will you require other responsibilities besides caring for the baby, such as cleaning, cooking, or taking the baby to the doctor? Do you have other children to care for as well? List all of your requirements so the candidate fully understands your needs before taking the job.

5. **Meet and greet the baby.** A good way to find out how the candidate gets along with your baby is to have him or her spend time with you and the baby. Observe how they get along and how comfortable he or she is with caring for your baby.

It worked for me!

"Show up unexpectedly. That is how I caught that guy smoking a cigar around my nine-month-old. When a child is upset about going to day care, don't ignore it!"

—Audra, Elliottsburg, Pennsylvania

WE ASKED: What top tips, tricks, and bits of advice would you give to a mom who is about to bring home multiples of her own?

"God bless you folks!"

—*Sarah, Kindsbach, New Jersey*

Baby, Oh Baby, Oh . . . Another Baby?

According to the National Center for Health Statistics, the twin birth rate has risen 55 percent since 1980. Triplets and quadruplets are on the rise, too, and a few moms of multiplies have even been on the *Today* show. Whether you've logged on a lot of miles on your double stroller or you're just trying to figure out how to change all those diapers in one day, you've got your hands full. I didn't have multiples (though I do have multiple kids here after school, most of whom aren't mine), so I will let MommaSaid's moms of multiples supply the tips here.

Five Tips for Parenting Multiple Babies

1. "Make diaper stations on every floor of your home! It will keep you from running around later."

   —*Kelsey, Coralville, Iowa*

2. "Have someone you trust come by to give you a break, do the laundry and dishes, and maybe cook some dinners that can be frozen and reheated later."

   —*Michelle, Simsboro, Louisiana*

3. "Start and stay on a routine. My boys will be two years old next week, and believe it or not, they tell me when it's time to go 'night-night.' I cannot stress enough that a routine can remove so much stress in your daily life."

—*Merin, Edmond, Oklahoma*

4. "Resist comparing them, even if they are identicals. It's tough, and you can't always help it, but resist it with all your might!"

—*Erin, Jacksonville, Florida*

5. "Ask for help . . . OFTEN."

—*Denise, Belleville, New Jersey*

"Make sure that you have someone you can call if you feel overwhelmed."

—*Jennifer, Edgewater, Maryland*

It worked for me!

"I cannot stress enough that a routine can remove so much stress in your daily life. And with multiples, you got stress! Also, don't worry about giving one more attention than the other. They will take care of that all by themselves!"

—*Merin, Edmond, Oklahoma*

It worked for me!

You're On Your Own

Whether you're a single mother or Daddy's gone a lot for work or in the military, parenting a baby on your own can be especially tough. When I was little, my father traveled two weeks out of every month for business, leaving my mom to take care of all things kids. Luckily, we lived next-door to my grandparents, who lived next-door to my aunt and uncle, so my mom had a built-in network of help. But even if you don't have family around to help, you can make parenting on your own easier. Here's how.

Five Tips for Parenting Baby on Your Own

1. **Turn to your family.** If your family lives nearby, make arrangements for regular help. Let Grandma and Grandpa take the baby, so you can go get a haircut or go back to school. Train an older niece or nephew to be a mother's helper. Ask your brother or sister to take the baby with them to the supermarket or Lowe's, so you can get a break.

2. **Find a support group.** Whether it's an online group or a meeting of local moms, find other mothers in the same situation as you. They'll not only have tips for parenting alone, they'll be great sounding boards for your issues and concerns.

3. **Don't try to do it all.** Parenting is hard enough for just one person to handle. You can't do it all, and you shouldn't try. Pick out what's most important to you, such as Mommy &

Me classes or baby snuggling time, and focus on that. It's better to be good at a few things than not-so-good at everything.

4. **Hire a sitter.** Sometimes, you'll need someone who's not family that you can rely on when you need help. Maybe your sister is getting married and your baby is the only family member who isn't invited. Or perhaps you want to save the family favors for big events, like your anniversary dinner, rather than your usual date night with Hubby. Find a good sitter you can call whenever you need someone to watch the baby. Ask neighbors for recommendations. You might even find someone who needs part-time help with whom you can share a sitter.

5. **Make time for yourself.** That's no small feat when you don't have a partner around to help out. But use some sitter time or family help, so you can go do something for yourself—and I don't mean researching cribs at Babies "R" Us. If you take a real break, you'll be a more rested, content mother.

Okay, I admit it. . . .

"I'm a military wife whose husband is gone a lot. It does totally stink to be the only one to guide your child, but hopefully you have neighbors, friends, and relatives to help a little bit."

—*Maura, Bettendorf, Iowa*

> "Don't apologize for being single, and don't try to be all things to your children. Be yourself, be true to them, and they will love you!"
>
> **It worked for me!**
>
> —*Merin, Edmond, Oklahoma*

When You're Separated or Divorced

Speaking of single parents, if you're separated or divorced, know that you're not alone. About twenty million children are being raised by single parents, but parenting a baby after a marriage dissolves has its own concerns. Here are some tips for handling them.

Five Tips for Parenting a Baby After Separation or Divorce

1. **Don't refer to Daddy as an idiot.** Your baby might not understand the meaning of "no good, cheating slimeball," but she will soon understand the sentiment. No matter how you feel about your ex right now, keep your bad feelings about Daddy to yourself. After all, he's her father, even if he's not part of your household anymore.

2. **Maintain structure.** If you're going through a separation and/or divorce with a baby in the house, try to keep his days as routine as possible. Babies can sense when you're upset, so maintaining structure will help assure your baby that, no matter what's happening between Mommy and Daddy, everything will be okay.

3. **Don't let the rules slide.** Now isn't the time to let go of the rules and cater to your baby's every whim. Even if Daddy spoils your baby, she still needs structure and boundaries just as much now as she did before the divorce or separation.

4. **Keep your baby's age in mind.** Babies under six months old have a hard time bonding with people they don't see often, because they simply don't remember for very long. Older babies sometimes experience stranger anxiety, acting fearful around the parent they don't see as often. It's up to you to – and the courts – to make sure that your baby has adequate visitation time with a noncustodial parent. The more you communicate with your ex, the more smoothly these visits will go.

5. **Let go of the bad feelings.** You don't need to turn every little transgression into a battle zone. The more realistic and relaxed you are, the better it is for your baby.

> **It worked for me!**
>
> "Find a sitter, friend, family member that will allow overnights for your baby (that you trust, obviously). Remember that you are a person with needs and wants, too."
>
> —Jennifer, Colorado Springs, Colorado

When Mommy's Sick

It's one thing to take care of a baby when you have a rotten cold and quite another when you have a chronic disease, such as multiple sclerosis or cancer. I've parented through chronic pain from endometriosis and lymphoma, so I know firsthand how difficult it can be when you're a mom who's chronically ill. Here are some of my tips

Okay, I admit it. . . .

"Relaxing is a silly word. Just take it all as it comes."

—*Nichole, Chandler, Arizona*

Five Tips for Parenting a Baby When You're Chronically Ill

1. **Accept the new you.** Before you were sick, you could get more done than you can now. Adding a baby to the mix makes it all the more difficult to maintain the status quo. But running yourself into the ground while you try to be "Perfect Mommy" doesn't do anyone any good, least of all your baby—or your health. You're a new mom with a special set of circumstances. Once you accept that, it'll be easier to get by.

2. **Ask for help.** Don't be afraid to ask relatives, neighbors, and friends to help care for your baby, so you can rest. I learned that when you're seriously ill, people want to help, and there's nothing wrong with asking for it or accepting it. The more your baby can keep his usual schedule, the better it is for him.

3. **Hug and kiss a lot.** Your baby needs it, and so do you. Though your baby is too young to comprehend your illness, she understands love. Whenever you have the strength, shower your baby with affection, because it's therapeutic for both of you.

4. **Don't go out if you can't handle it.** Your baby is happiest being with you. So don't push yourself to take him out to the park or to mom-baby classes when you're too weak. You'll only set yourself back, making it harder for you to care for your baby at home. Conserve your energy and use it wisely.

5. **Give your baby as much attention as you can.** If that means you sit by the playpen and coo, that's plenty. You don't have to put on a big show or make teachable moments out of breakfast to be in your baby's life. Just be there, and be yourself. That's plenty.

Okay, I admit it. . . .

"I wish someone would have told me that no one is perfect—that being a parent is a different experience for everyone."

—*Suz, Longwood, Florida*

Which One of These Is Not Like the Others?

Whatever your special situation, seek out other people who are going through or who have been through the same thing as you.

You'll feel much better when you can share your concerns and issues with someone who truly understands what it's like to be in your shoes. On the Internet, you'll find groups that offer support both online and in person, and there are lots of books about your specific issue on the shelves at your local library or bookstore. If you need one-on-one help with a serious issue, consider seeing a trained counselor. Whatever you do, remember that your baby loves you no matter what.

WE ASKED: What's your favorite part about parenting babies?

"The unconditional love without the whining."

—Lissa, Spring Mills, Pennsylvania

Gimme a break

Juggling Baby with Work

If you've gone back to work since your baby was born, you're no doubt trying to figure out the "secret" to balancing it all. Okay, here's the secret: there is no secret. There's no one way to juggle motherhood with work. What's more, the whole issue changes as your child gets older. For instance, the nanny you rely on to watch your baby might not be needed in a few years. Or you may decide you're not happy with the after-care program at school. Or you might decide to work from home. As your child and your situation change, your plans will, too. Stop trying to find the secret, and focus on finding what works for you and your family now.

Just a minute!

Baby's First Year Exit Interview

1. What is your primary reason for leaving?

   My kid becomes a toddler tomorrow. Besides, I've stocked up on Pull-Ups, I've ditched the bottles, and we've enrolled in the "walkers" class at Mom and Tot.

2. Did anything trigger your decision to leave?

   Yes, my breasts stopped leaking, and I got back into my prepregnancy jeans.

3. What was the most satisfying part of Baby's first year?

   The first time he smiled at me—and it wasn't just gas.

4. What was the least satisfying part of Baby's first year?

   I was awake for too much of it.

5. Did your duties turn out as you expected?

   If somebody had told me that I'd figure out how to open a stroller with one hand, hold a squirming baby with the other, and text Hubby to bring home teething meds all at the same time, I wouldn't have believed it, anyhow.

6. Did you receive enough training to do your job well?

   Exactly how do you train for surreptitiously breast-feeding in front of squeamish family members while chitchatting about potato salad?

7. Did you receive adequate feedback about your performance?

   Only the baby greets me as though Elvis has just arrived in Graceland, so yeah.

8. Can we do anything to encourage you to stay?

   Nah. Unless, of course, my pregnancy test comes back positive. . . .

Bye-Bye

So, there you have it—everything I would tell you about parenting babies if we met at the back fence. I hope you got a lot out of all the mom-tested tips, the "been there" stories, and the much-needed, reassuring pats on the back.

Whether you're facing down colic, frantically baby-proofing before your newly crawling baby gets there first, or are just plain wiped out, remember: you're not the only one going through it, no matter how lonely it feels at times. Whenever you need a pick-me-up, advice, or something other than baby talk, flip through this guide or drop by MommaSaid.net for laughs and validation. We're always here for you, even if your baby just skipped nap time altogether.

Okay, I admit it. . . .

"I love watching every milestone. Each day brings something new and different, something exciting, challenging, or eventful (even if it is just a BM).

—*Kristen, Modesto, California*

Index

Confident Parenting
during the Toddler Years

Code # 6535 • Paperback • $14.95

In *Stop Second-Guessing Yourself: The Toddler Years*, award-winning website creator and blogger Jen Singer offers the same camaraderie, advice, and encouragement she's become known for as the Internet's favorite Momma. Filled with proven real-world parenting tips, moms' true confessions, and plenty of humor, this validating guide will help you survive the toddler years with more confidence. It's the field guide to confident parenting that you'll want to keep in the diaper bag, just in case.

Confident Parenting during the Preschool Years

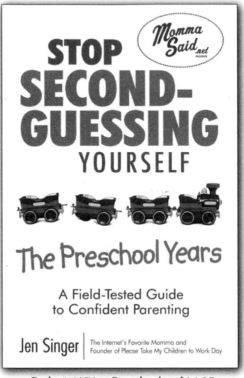

In *Stop Second-Guessing Yourself: The Preschool Years,* Jen Singer, "The Internet's Favorite Momma," shares her must-know advice plus dozens of "what works" tips from other moms. In this manifesto for modern momhood, she gives the girlfriendly skinny on everything that could confound you during the preschool years, from sleep issues to sibling rivalry, from starting school to stopping whining, from potty-training to picky eaters. With candid confessions, prescriptive tips, and a much-needed dose of humor, this must-have resource will help moms like you lose the doubt and gain much-needed advice and a pat on the back.

3 1901 04939 2915